Composing *Yourself*

A Student Guide to Introductory Composition at Purdue

2012 – 2013

SAMANTHA BLACKMON

LINDA HAYNES

LAURIE A. PINKERT

As a textbook publisher, we are faced with enormous environmental issues due to the large amount of paper contained in our print products. Since our inception in 2002, we have worked diligently to be as eco-friendly as possible.

Our green initiatives include:

Electronic Products
We deliver products in non-paper form whenever possible. This includes pdf downloadables, flash drives, and CDs.

Electronic Samples
We use Xample, a new electronic sampling system. Instructor samples are sent via a personalized web page that links to pdf downloads.

FSC Certified Printers
All of our printers are certified by the Forest Service Council which promotes environmentally and socially responsible management of the world's forests. This program allows consumer groups, individual consumers, and businesses to work together hand-in-hand to promote responsible use of the world's forests as a renewable and sustainable resource.

Recycled Paper
Most of our products are printed on a minimum of 30% post-consumer waste recycled paper.

Support of Green Causes
When we do print, we donate a portion of our revenue to green causes. Listed below are a few of the organizations that have received donations from Fountainhead Press. We welcome your feedback and suggestions for contributions, as we are always searching for worthy initiatives.

Rainforest 2 Reef

Environmental Working Group

Cover image by Frank Tobienne

Cover design by Ellie Moore

Text design by Deborah M. Lindberg

Books may be purchased for educational purposes.

For information, please call or write:

1-800-586-0330
Fountainhead Press
2140 E. Southlake Blvd., Suite L #816
Southlake, TX 76092
Web site: www. fountainheadpress.com
E-mail: customerservice@fountainheadpress.com

ISBN 978-1-59871-555-2

Printed in the United States of America

Composing *Yourself*

A Student Guide to Introductory Composition at Purdue

2012 – 2013

SAMANTHA BLACKMON

LINDA HAYNES

LAURIE A. PINKERT

Acknowledgments

Special thanks to Terrance Manning whose peer review worksheets were adapted for this book and to Chelsea Stripe who compiled the Purdue Libraries information that was adapted for the secondary research section. Purdue University Libraries information was excerpted and adapted from the Purdue University Libraries website and its CORE tutorials. For additional or updated information and tutorials, visit http://www.lib.purdue.edu/. All syllabus approach descriptions were excerpted from the ICaP website and were written and revised by past and present members of the approaches.

The cover image "The Demiurgic: *Composing Rhetorica*" is an original painting by Francis Tobienne, Jr. Professor Tobienne was born and raised on the beautiful island of St. Croix, Virgin Islands; educated in the Midwest and trained as a medievalist at Purdue University, West Lafayette—Indiana; moreover, Tobienne continues his intellectual pursuits as a scientist, artist, poet, author, lecturer and currently teaches Literature, Intellectual History and Theory at University of South Florida—St. Petersburg campus as both a Purdue Doctoral Fellow and Dalí Research Fellow. On the heels of his first book: *The Position of Magic In Selected Medieval Spanish Texts* (Cambridge: Cambridge Scholars Publishing, 2008), Tobienne's second monograph project: *Dalí's Medievalism: La Brujería de las Mujeres* is forthcoming.

All efforts were made to ensure that web addresses and links referenced in this text were current at the time of publication; however, readers may find that some links have changed since the publication date.

Contents

What Resources Are Available to Me?   3

What Software and New Technologies Will I Need to Use/Learn?   4

What Should I Know about Research and Writing?   5

Where Can I Publish My ICaP Work?   6

What ICaP and Purdue Policies Should I Know?   7

Appendix   A

Introduction:
How Can I Use *Composing Yourself?*

Introduction to This Book

Composing Yourself is a bit of a hybrid text. It is simultaneously a handbook that will introduce you to the policies and procedures of the Introductory Composition program at Purdue University, a storehouse for forms that you will need for your Composition class, and a calendar template you can develop using items from the included list of important official university dates and as a place to write in the due dates for all of your assignments and project deadlines. While this book is specifically for students taking classes in ICaP (Introductory Composition at Purdue) it can be useful for all of your classes. *(It is also quite stylish.)* *Composing Yourself* is aimed at making your ICaP experience a smooth one. Most of the documents and answers that you need are contained within this book and your instructor will likely refer to it on a regular basis.

The following chapter will give you an introduction to ICaP and the courses we offer, information about the goals of each of the courses, and a list of approaches to and textbooks used in the ICaP courses. In Chapter 2 you will find information on how your ICaP courses will be different from other English courses you have taken in high school, grades and grading policies, and a bit about what makes your writing course different from other writing courses. Chapter 3 helps you figure out what resources are available to you for help with everything from a draft of your paper to getting your computer to cooperate as you are doing everything from checking email to editing video. Chapter 4 talks specifically about some of the technologies that will be used in your class and how they will be used. There are also some resources to help get you started. Chapter 5 offers some great resources of research and writing such as where to go to do research, addresses the question of what counts as research, and helps you figure out how to use that research in a composition exercise. Chapter 6 details a list of venues you can use to share your work with the world at local levels and beyond. Chapter 7 gives the specifics of a myriad of university and ICaP policies to make your time in our program (and at the university) run as smoothly as possible. The last section of this book is an Appendix of perforated forms that you can tear out and use over the course of the semester.

Knowing When It's Due:
Filling Out Your Course Calendar

One of the ways that you can use *Composing Yourself* is to keep track of your assignments and your grades. To help you do this, we've provided the calendar below that you can fill in throughout the semester. At the beginning of the semester, you should receive a list of due dates or a course calendar from your instructor. The dates may be distributed in print or as an online document on your course site, and you should reference those dates throughout the semester. This calendar is for your use. You can use it to record your daily assignments and to add due dates that your instructor has provided.

To get you started, we've provided some important dates from the Purdue Academic Calendar that you can add for yourself.

2012–2013
SELECTED PURDUE ACADEMIC CALENDAR DATES

Fall 2012

Monday	August 20	Classes Begin
Friday	August 24	Last Day for Late Registration
Monday	September 3	Labor Day—No Classes
Monday	September 3	Last day to cancel a course without it appearing on record
Monday	September 17	Last Day to withdraw with a grade of W
Mon–Tues	October 8-9	Fall Break—No Classes
Wed-Sat	November 21-24	Thanksgiving Break—No Classes
Saturday	December 8	Classes End
Mon–Sat	December 10-15	Final Exams

Spring 2013

Monday	January 7	Classes Begin
Friday	January 11	Last Day for Late Registration
Monday	January 21	Last day to cancel a course without it appearing on record
Monday	February 4	Last Day to withdraw with a grade of W
Mon–Sat	March 11–16	Spring Vacation—No Classes
Saturday	April 27	Classes End
Mon–Sat	April 29–May 4	Final Exams

	Week 1	Week 2	Week 3	Week 4
Weekend				
Friday				
Thursday				
Wednesday				
Tuesday				
Monday				

	Monday	Tuesday	Wednesday	Thursday	Friday	Weekend
Week 5						
Week 6						
Week 7						
Week 8						

Weekend	Friday	Thursday	Wednesday	Tuesday	Monday	
						Week 9
						Week 10
						Week 11
						Week 12

	Week 13	Week 14	Week 15	Week 16
Monday				
Tuesday				
Wednesday				
Thursday				
Friday				
Weekend				

Tracking Your Progress: Composing Your Own Gradebook

As a college student, you need to take responsibility for tracking your progress in your courses. Although your instructors should communicate clearly about your grade on a particular assignment, they won't necessarily be able to calculate your course average on the spot. Additionally, many ICaP courses involve a number of daily writing assignments or in-class activities for which you receive credit/no credit rather than a numeric grade. You'll want to keep track of these assignments as you complete them.

To provide a place for you to keep track of your own grades throughout the semester, we've included the chart below. Fill in the assignment titles or dates and the grade/credit you earned. This will help you track your progress throughout the semester.

Assignment Title or Date	Credit Earned or Grade Received	Percentage of Total Course Credit
Sample: Literacy Narrative	80	20%
Sample: Journal Assignment	X	

1

What Is ICaP
(Introductory Composition at Purdue)?

THE GOAL: BY THE END OF THIS CHAPTER, YOU'LL KNOW WHAT ICaP STANDS FOR; WHAT ITS GOALS, MEANS, AND OUTCOMES ARE; WHAT COURSES ICaP OFFERS, AND THE GENERAL STRUCTURE FOR YOUR SELECTED ICaP COURSE.

What Is ICaP (Introductory Composition at Purdue)?

Writing plays a central role in the ability to communicate within and outside the university. Therefore, Introductory Composition at Purdue (ICaP) is a program designed to help students:

- build confidence in their abilities to create, interpret, and evaluate texts in all types of media;
- develop knowledge by inspiring new ideas through writing;
- understand, evaluate, and organize ideas;
- articulate, develop, and support a topic through first-hand and archival research; and
- respond credibly and accurately to a variety of writing situations.

REGARDLESS OF YOUR ACADEMIC INTERESTS, PROFESSIONAL GOALS, OR PARTICULAR FIELD OF STUDY, THE ABILITY TO COMMUNICATE CREATIVELY AND EFFECTIVELY IS IMPORTANT.

Regardless of your academic interests, professional goals, or particular field of study, the ability to communicate creatively and effectively is important for several reasons: 1) it provides an outlet for sharing ideas and an opportunity for making those ideas better; 2) it empowers you to understand different conventions, genres, groups, societies, and cultures; and 3) it allows you to have a voice in multiple academic, civic, and personal situations. In short, writing is a way of learning that spans all fields and disciplines, and your ICaP course will help you learn how to write more effectively in the various situations that you may encounter during your undergraduate years and beyond.

The ICaP program offers four different first year courses that meet the same university composition requirement. These four courses—First Year Composition (10600), Lilly Learning Community First Year Composition (10600-R), First Year Composition for International Students (10600-I), and Accelerated Composition: Engaging in Public Discourse (10800)—which will be discussed in detail later in this chapter, share common instructional methods and meet common goals in order to ensure that no matter which ICaP course you take, you will be able to meet the course outcomes and have the opportunity to become a more effective writer.

Shared Goals

Sometimes ICaP courses can seem pretty different on the surface—one class might require students to create a documentary film while another might involve web design; one class might integrate comic books into the course reading list while another might require you to read a novel. Although the differences are what people may notice at first, there are actually more similarities than differences among ICaP courses. It's important to remember that even though the specific theme or approach of your composition class may differ from another's, all ICaP courses meet a set of shared program goals. Your instructor has designed your particular course—the readings, the writing projects, the in-class activities, the peer reviews, etc.—to meet these shared goals in a certain way.

The ICaP course goals, which you will be working toward throughout the semester, can be grouped into the following categories: (1) rhetorical knowledge, (2) critical thinking, reading, and writing, (3) writing processes, (4) knowledge of conventions, and (5) technology. Meeting the goals in each of these categories will require that you not only complete your assigned writing projects but also that you engage in class activities and reading assignments. For this reason, you'll find that your attendance in class and your daily reading/writing assignments may be emphasized in your ICaP class in a way that they are not emphasized in your other courses. It's important to remember that meeting your ICaP course goals isn't just about turning in "good papers"; it's about participating in a learning process throughout the entire semester.

> **MEETING YOUR ICaP COURSE GOALS ISN'T JUST ABOUT TURNING IN "GOOD PAPERS"; IT'S ABOUT PARTICIPATING IN A LEARNING PROCESS THROUGHOUT THE ENTIRE SEMESTER.**

RHETORICAL KNOWLEDGE GOALS

ICaP's rhetorical knowledge goals aim to help students effectively understand the role that writing plays in various situations and the influence that a situation can have on the choices that writers make during the writing process. These rhetorical knowledge goals include: (1) to help students understand the inherent rhetorical situation of writing including purpose, audience, and context; (2) to prepare students for writing in later university courses across the curriculum by helping them learn to articulate, develop, and support a point through both primary and secondary research; and (3) to help students understand that they can and should use writing for multiple academic, civic, professional, and personal purposes.

Throughout the semester, your course instructor will introduce you to a variety of writing assignments that accomplish different purposes, reach different audiences, and use different media. Practice with a variety of writing tasks will help you understand how writing can be used for different purposes and how every writing occasion is shaped by a particular purpose, audience, and context. Additionally, within your various writing tasks, you will learn how to connect your research about a topic with your own developing ideas on that topic. Whether you're analyzing a text and need to situate your analysis within a larger conversation or you're conducting interviews to gather new information on a topic that has not previously been studied, your research in your ICaP course should help you learn how to credibly develop and support your conclusions.

CRITICAL THINKING, READING, AND WRITING GOALS

ICaP's critical thinking, reading, and writing goals are two-fold: (1) to provide students with opportunities to write as a means of discovery and learning about themselves; as an integral part of inquiry about the material, social, and cultural contexts they share with others; and as a means of exploring, understanding, and evaluating ideas in academic disciplines; and (2) to help students develop their abilities to create, interpret and evaluate a variety of types of texts integrating verbal and visual components.

The first goal involves the ability to think about a situation or topic from various perspectives. Although this process of critical engagement will certainly involve articulating and understanding your own personal experiences, you will also need to consider situations or topics from others' perspectives, too. Learning to see things from others' perspectives is something that requires more than just your own ability to write—it involves listening, thinking, and reflecting. For this reason, your instructor may often ask you to participate in discussions with your peers or to reflect on your own and others' writing throughout the semester.

The second goal—creating, interpreting, and evaluating a variety of texts—highlights the fact that writing doesn't happen only in words. You might be thinking, "What do you mean?! Of course, writing happens in words." However, if you take a minute to think about your daily activities and interactions, you'll quickly see that writing or communication happens through text on a computer screen, images in a magazine, and sound bytes on the internet. This second goal aims to help you see the ways that these different kinds of writing (or *composing,* as we often describe it in the ICaP program) can be used to communicate different kinds of information or can be used for different purposes. For instance, imagine you've been assigned the task of teaching a group of elementary school students about a new recycling program that's beginning at their school. You probably won't write an 8–10 page paper detailing the program and its benefits; instead, you'll create posters or a game to help students visualize and understand how to recycle. This goal of creating, interpreting, and evaluating a variety of texts isn't just about writing that happens outside of the university either. If you open a research journal in your field, it's likely that you'll see tables, charts, graphs, or pictures to describe a scientific experiment or report research data. Understanding the ways that visuals work and how you can create such visuals is just one of the ways that this goal, which will help you both in and out of the classroom, can be met.

IF YOU TAKE A MINUTE TO THINK ABOUT YOUR DAILY ACTIVITIES AND INTERACTIONS, YOU'LL SEE THAT WRITING OR COMMUNICATION HAPPENS THROUGH TEXT ON A COMPUTER SCREEN, IMAGES IN A MAGAZINE, AND SOUND BYTES ON THE INTERNET.

WRITING PROCESSES GOAL

The writing process goal aims to help students develop effective and efficient processes for writing by providing practice with planning, drafting, revising, and editing their writing in multiple genres using a variety of media. Meeting this goal will require that you not just turn in a polished final draft on the day that your writing project is due but rather that you learn how to plan and draft in advance and how to integrate peer and instructor feedback to strengthen your writing projects.

KNOWLEDGE OF CONVENTIONS GOALS

The knowledge of conventions goals are the ones that most students in ICaP courses associate with their previous English courses. These goals aim (1) to introduce students to the conventions of form, style, and citation and documentation of sources that are appropriate to their purposes for composing in a variety of media for a variety of rhetorical contexts and (2) to demonstrate that coherent structure, effective style, and grammatical and mechanical correctness contribute to a writer's credibility and authority.

In the ICaP program these knowledge of conventions goals will not just teach you to memorize the conventions as rules but will help you to understand why discourse conventions are important and how to connect the conventions to the audience expectations. That is, you'll learn to see how the conventions change based on the audience to which you're writing and the genre that you're using. For example, a letter to the editor will use different conventions than an essay to your professor.

TECHNOLOGY GOAL

As you already know, writing in today's world takes a variety of shapes. As a college student, you might write on sticky-notes, update your Facebook page, and scribble on your hand before breakfast, and then you might text a friend, send an e-mail, and type a paper for your history class before lunch. Composing in various technologies is something that you'll do in college and something that won't change when you enter the real world. As an employee, you might be designing PowerPoint presentations for a company, giving public lectures for your non-profit organization, or writing instructions for a piece of equipment in your shop. For this reason, ICaP's technology goal aims to provide students with experience using multiple composing technologies to produce a variety of genres of texts. Because student experiences are so diverse and software changes so rapidly, your ICaP course can't teach you every technology or software that you will use in the future. What it can do, however, is teach you how to develop the skills you'll need to learn new technologies and to use them effectively.

COMPOSING IN VARIOUS TECHNOLOGIES IS SOMETHING THAT YOU'LL DO IN COLLEGE AND SOMETHING THAT WON'T CHANGE WHEN YOU ENTER THE REAL WORLD.

As you can see from these categories and goals, ICaP course goals can't be met just by turning in a set of traditional double-spaced MLA style papers. These goals require you to engage in a learning process throughout the semester that involves class activities, critical engagement in course materials, developing a writing process, and working in various technologies that are appropriate to your course projects.

ICaP Goals

Rhetorical Knowledge	To help students understand the inherent rhetorical situation of writing including purpose, audience, and context.
	To prepare students for writing in later university courses across the curriculum by helping them learn to articulate, develop, and support a point through both primary and secondary research.
	To help students understand that they can and should use writing for multiple academic, civic, professional, and personal purposes.
Critical Thinking, Reading, and Writing	To provide students with opportunities to write as a means of discovery and learning about themselves; as an integral part of inquiry about the material, social, and cultural contexts they share with others; and as a means of exploring, understanding, and evaluating ideas in academic disciplines.
	To help students develop their abilities to create, interpret and evaluate a variety of types of texts integrating verbal and visual components.
Writing Process	To help students develop effective and efficient processes for writing by providing practice with planning, drafting, revising, and editing their writing in multiple genres using a variety of media.
Knowledge of Conventions	To introduce students to the conventions of form, style, and citation and documentation of sources that are appropriate to their purposes for composing in a variety of media for a variety of rhetorical contexts.
	To demonstrate that coherent structure, effective style, and grammatical and mechanical correctness contribute to a writer's credibility and authority.
Technology	To provide students with experience using multiple composing technologies to produce a variety of genres of texts.

Shared Means of Instruction and Shared Outcomes in ICaP Courses

Because ICaP courses have shared goals that they strive to meet, you can expect some shared means of instruction even though topics and themes may differ from course to course. These shared means of instruction include:

- Regular classroom instruction using a variety of modes for learning, including attending lectures, participating in class discussions, contributing to collaborative learning in small groups, and providing critiques of peers' writing.

- Integration of an online course site that includes your course syllabus and may involve regular online discussions or blog posts.

- Completion of textual interpretation and production assignments in a variety of genres and a variety of media, including print, computer-mediated, and mass media.

- Frequent, periodic review of and commentary on successive drafts of writing projects by peers and instructor.

- Production of 7,500–11,500 words of polished writing (or 15,000–22,000 words, including drafts) or the equivalent.

With common goals and common means of instruction, all students—regardless of the specific topics their composition course may engage—should achieve similar outcomes. By the end of an ICaP course, students should be able to:

- Demonstrate familiarity with concepts used to describe writing processes (planning, drafting, revising, editing, and proofreading) and effectively use variation of these processes in their writing.
  - Use appropriate and effective planning and organizing strategies.
  - Evaluate others' commentary on early drafts and incorporate useful suggestions into subsequent drafts.
  - Edit and proofread their papers to maximize their credibility and authority.

- Identify and state the purpose of a writing task they have completed.

- Adapt their writing in ways appropriate for different audiences.

- Explain why a piece of writing is or is not effective and suggest strategies for improvement.
  - Effectively evaluate others' writing and provide useful commentary and suggestions for revision where appropriate.

- Distinguish among conventions for citing and documenting sources in various genres and various media for various audiences.
- Make stylistic changes to improve the effectiveness of their writing.
- Demonstrate an understanding of the basic elements of visual rhetoric.
  - Know how to use commonplace software to create visuals that effectively make or support arguments.
  - Distinguish between information that is best communicated in visual format and information best communicated in text and make transitions and connections between visual and textual elements.
  - Be able to critique visual designs and formats.

Introductory Courses

To help students develop as writers and to meet the ICaP goals, means, and outcomes, the ICaP program offers four introductory courses and one advanced course:

English 10600	First Year Composition
English 10600-R	Lilly Learning Community First Year Composition
English 10600-I	International First Year Composition
English 10800	Accelerated Composition: Engaging in Public Discourse
English 30400	Advanced Composition

FIRST YEAR COMPOSITION (ENGLISH 10600)

English 10600 is the standard 4-credit hour composition course for students entering Purdue. In this course, you will meet weekly in both a traditional classroom space and in a computer lab. Additionally, you will meet weekly or bi-weekly in one-to-one or small group writing conference with your instructor.

Your writing topics will be closely tied to the course's theme or approach. (For more information about the various syllabus approaches, see pages 13–17.) Your writing topics may include personal experiences, research-based arguments, and/or topics that are related to your major field of study. You may also spend some time exploring rhetorical contexts, and producing, interpreting, and analyzing multimedia environments. No matter which topics your course investigates, you will be required to conduct different types of research and may create a final project that demonstrates the expertise you have gained over the semester. As such, your instructor may use planning assignments in order to help you discover and explore a topic, perspective, or audience.

In addition to writing throughout the course, you will also spend significant time reading. You can expect to read and discuss writing by you, your peers, and professionals. Such shared readings and discussions may take place through in-class review sessions or bi-weekly conferences. Additionally, your instructors may select outside readings related to the theme of the class or similar in purpose to the writing they expect you to do.

LILLY LEARNING COMMUNITY FIRST YEAR COMPOSITION (ENGLISH 10600-R)

Sections of English 10600-R are designated as part of a Lilly Learning Community, which means that the introductory composition course is paired with another course that students take. Thus, the same set of students should be enrolled in two of the same courses. The Learning Community (LC) introductory composition course takes the same course format as traditional 106 classes—meeting twice a week in a traditional classroom, once a week in a computer lab, and weekly or biweekly in a conference setting.

These courses often integrate content topics from the paired course. For example, in a Biology LC students may read scientific articles about a particular topic in their Biology class. Then, in the composition course, they might re-examine the same articles to understand how biologists conduct research and how they write about their research. Such analysis would use the same article from the Biology course but would examine this article in a different way in order to meet the goals of the composition course.

In addition to having overlapping course content, students in a Learning Community section can expect to participate in extracurricular activities. Sometimes these activities will be socially-focused, bringing together students for dinner or an outing. Other times, these activities will be educationally focused. For instance, Hospitality and Tourism Management students might take a trip to a Chicago restaurant and meet with a chef in order to see the restaurant practices firsthand. If you are enrolled in a Learning Community you can expect that your instructors for both of the courses in the LC meet regularly throughout the semester to discuss their coordinating topics and activities.

INTERNATIONAL FIRST YEAR COMPOSITION (ENGLISH 10600-I)

Sections of English 10600 which have an "I" in the section number are reserved for speakers of English as a second language. These sections of first-year composition have the same prerequisites, fulfill the same requirements, and are similar to other sections of English 10600 in aim, content, and structure. Like the other 10600 courses, 10600-I sections integrate both the traditional classroom setting, the one-to-one or small group conference, and computer-based instruction; however, the weekly rotation of these instructional methods is more flexible in 10600-I; therefore, course instructors can adjust the method of instruction based on writers' needs. These courses are capped at 15 students (contrasting the 20-student enrollment cap of other introductory courses), allowing instructors to devote more time to commenting on students' papers and providing focused instruction.

Instructors of 10600-I courses receive additional preparation in order to meet the unique cultural and linguistic needs of second-language writers. Additionally, the curriculum is designed so that the writers develop a growing expertise on a selected topic throughout the semester. If you enroll in a 10600-I course, you can expect to select a topic at the beginning of the semester that you will write about from various angles and using various research methods throughout the semester. You can also expect to write three drafts of every writing project and to receive instructor comments on the first two drafts before the final draft receives a grade.

ACCELERATED COMPOSITION: ENGAGING IN PUBLIC DISCOURSE (ENGLISH 10800)

English 10800 is a 3-credit accelerated introductory composition course in which students will engage in public writing and community service. The purpose of integrating a service-learning component into this introductory course is three-fold: (1) to increase students' awareness of the rhetorical strategies integral for the composition of effective written, visual, and multimedia texts, (2) to develop students' understanding of what service learning is and how it relates both to education more generally and one's own life more specifically, and (3) to introduce students to the larger, local community in which they live, beyond Purdue's campus borders. This course emphasizes a rigorous approach with high expectations on students' abilities to work quickly and independently.

If you enroll in this class, you can expect to work at a faster pace and to read and write more than your peers enrolled in English 10600. As you engage in local community activities outside the classroom, you will also complete writing assignments in collaboration with your community partner. Some of this text production may be done using multimedia, and some of it may be composed in short assignments. To successfully complete this class, you should have experience in completing complex, research-based writing projects, and also have fluent control of discourse conventions such as sentence structure, punctuation, spelling, and mechanics.

AS YOU ENGAGE IN LOCAL COMMUNITY ACTIVITIES OUTSIDE THE CLASSROOM, YOU WILL ALSO COMPLETE WRITING ASSIGNMENTS IN COLLABORATION WITH YOUR COMMUNITY PARTNER.

ADVANCED COURSES: ENGLISH 30400

Currently, the ICaP program offers one advanced writing course: English 30400. This Advanced Composition course focuses on non-fictional, non-narrative composition. The course includes study and class discussion of rhetorical theories, principles and models. Students can expect to learn about writing conventions in their own disciplines through reading and writing assignments that require analysis and research. Students can also expect to gain extensive practice in stylistic and content revision. If you complete your first year course and find that you want to further develop your writing skills, you can enroll in this course for more focused attention on your reading, research, and writing abilities.

Enrolling in the Most Appropriate ICaP Course

Most students enroll in one of the ICaP courses in either Fall or Spring of their first year. Your academic advisor may have specific suggestions on which class you should take for your program. However, the following guidelines may help you in determining the appropriate course placement for you.

You should consider enrolling in First Year Composition (English 10600) if:

- Your SAT Critical Reading score is below 670 or your ACT English is below 30

- You think you would benefit from having individual conferences to discuss your writing

- You would welcome the chance to develop your writing skills in a computer lab classroom

- Establishing a solid academic foundation for college work is important to you

- You are an international student
  - with a total TOEFL score is 100 or above (internet-based test)
  - with a writing subscore is 26 or above (internet-based test)
  - who has used English as the medium of instruction in your education prior to Purdue
  - whose parents, sibling(s) or other family members attended a college or university
  - who will be able to handle a heavy (many pages) reading load
  - who is familiar with the informal written and spoken English often used in Purdue classes

You should consider enrolling in Lilly Learning Community First Year Composition (English 10600-R) if:

- You would like to participate in activities outside the classroom

- You are interested in a different kind of learning experience

- You would like to enhance your writing class with a paired class in your area

- You would like to attend two or three classes with the same group of students

- You have looked into the Learning Community opportunities on their website (http://www.purdue.edu/sats/learning_communities)

- You have talked with your academic advisor to find out if a Learning Community is right for you.

You should consider enrolling in International First Year Composition (English 10600-I) if:

- You speak English as a second language
- Your TOEFL total score is below 100 (internet-based test)
- Your TOEFL writing subscore is below 26 (internet-based test)
- English has not been the medium of instruction for most of your education prior to Purdue
- You are in the first generation of your family to attend a college or university
- Your speaking/listening skills in English are not as strong as your writing/reading
- You are likely to need extra time for and will have difficulty with a heavy reading load

You should consider enrolling in Accelerated Composition: Engaging in Public Discourse (English 10800) if:

- You usually try to exceed your instructor's expectations
- You are interested in **engaging in public writing**
- You are interested in **community service**
- You enjoy the challenge of an accelerated course
- Your SAT Critical Reading score is 670 or above or your ACT English is 30 or above
- You have fluent control of conventions such as sentence structure, punctuation, and mechanics
- You usually understand teachers' instructions the first time and rarely need repeated explanation
- You believe you are better prepared for college-level work than most first-year students

Regardless of which course you're enrolled in, you'll complete at least a short writing assignment within the first week of class, which your instructor will review in order to confirm that the course placement is appropriate. Typically, no matter what course they are enrolled in, students who complete the work of the course and address any concerns with the instructor in a timely manner find that they are able to meet the outcomes of the course. In rare cases, students may be encouraged to check the availability in another section/course or to take an ICaP course in a later semester.

Students who wish to move to a different course must do so within the first week of classes. Due to the important material covered at the beginning of ICaP courses, students are not permitted to move to a different section after the first week of class. That is, instructors cannot sign you into their classes after the period for online adding/dropping has lapsed. (For more information about add/drop procedures, please see Registration: Drop/Add Procedures in Section 7.)

Syllabus Approaches Used in First Year Composition (English 10600)

Themes and topics in English 10600 courses may vary depending on the syllabus approach that's integrated into the course. The approaches currently used in ICaP courses include the following:

- Academic Writing and Research
- Composing Through Literature
- Composing With Popular Culture
- Digital Rhetorics
- Documenting Realities
- UR@
- Writing About Writing
- Writing Your Way Into Purdue

For more information about these approaches and what you can expect in the courses within these approaches, read the corresponding description below.

ACADEMIC WRITING AND RESEARCH

The main goal of the Academic Writing and Research Approach is to help students situate themselves in the world of academic discourse. Thus, this approach has perhaps a more explicit and sustained focus on interpreting and producing text than other methods of teaching English 10600. Common assignments include literacy narratives, analyses of scholarly arguments, and writing arguments targeted to particular academic discourse communities. However, instructors in this approach can and do cover web writing and new media instruction in their courses, with the understanding that such skills are a part of contemporary academic and professional life. Moreover, they are committed to scaffolding student learning by sequencing assignments so that the skills learned during one assignment can be practiced in the remaining assignments.

Those who teach the Academic Writing and Research syllabus approach acknowledge that there is no single "academic" subject matter or style of writing; however, they seek to help students identify and understand the voice, genres, modes, and argumentative strategies preferred and privileged in many academic discourses. Instructors also teach students the importance of and strategies to deal with the complexities of academic research. Instructors also provide continual support as students learn to use all kinds of source material effectively and appropriately in their own writing. They understand that many students have not been exposed to academic discourse and need practice decoding and generating it. Instructors who have adopted this approach commonly explore the social and political dimensions of the academy's language bias.

COMPOSING THROUGH LITERATURE

The Composing Through Literature Syllabus Approach seeks to develop critical thinking and analytical skills in its students and to aid these students in articulating their original thoughts and arguments in textual, visual, and electronic documents. The premise of the syllabus approach is that students are well served by extensive exposure to written literature and engaging, complex texts that encourage critical analysis, thoughtful reflection, and a deep involvement with the significance of the written word. Literary texts also demand a high level of attention to detail, logical thought, audience awareness, and an understanding of narrative and subjective bias. Furthermore, such texts provide a high level of educational and stylistic examples to encourage the development of written prose.

> **...STUDENTS ARE WELL SERVED BY EXTENSIVE EXPOSURE TO WRITTEN LITERATURE AND ENGAGING, COMPLEX TEXTS THAT ENCOURAGE CRITICAL ANALYSIS, THOUGHTFUL REFLECTION, AND A DEEP INVOLVEMENT WITH THE SIGNIFICANCE OF THE WRITTEN WORD.**

This syllabus approach, though focusing primarily on traditional print literature, also turns the students' attention to music, art, advertising, film, comedy, and comics/graphic novels and teaches the students to think of these examples from other media as texts with an intended audience, argument, and purpose which can be analyzed both specifically and holistically in a way similar to a written work. The students are then asked to turn that same analytic gaze to their own work. The primary goal of this syllabus approach is that students will leave not only with the skills to analyze the written and visual materials that will be presented to them throughout the rest of their student careers and beyond but to also be capable of communicating their ideas about these materials efficiently and effectively in clear, well-developed prose.

COMPOSING THROUGH POP CULTURE

Composing with Popular Culture is a 106 syllabus approach that gives students the opportunity to rhetorically and critically engage with popular culture texts. Instructors in this approach emphasize the production and analysis of multimedia, multimodal and multigenre texts, combining the inquiry and research methods of traditional academic approaches with the participatory meaning-making practices advocated by fan studies theorists like Constance Penley, Camille Bacon-Smith, Henry Jenkins, and Rhiannon Bury.

Assignments encourage students to rhetorically situate popular culture texts through a variety of perspectives, including critical, participatory, audience, and genre. Through the utilization of a variety of new media tools, students are encouraged to reach, impact, and interact with actual audiences and rhetorical situations while simultaneously experiencing the historically access-restricted role of being a cultural producer. Our goal is ultimately to use the sites of popular culture to focus on teaching composition as a reciprocal and dynamic process of participation between composer, audience, and culture(s). We encourage students to see culture as a network of texts that creates both knowledge and identity by virtue of interacting with (and contributing to) it in a rhetorically-grounded manner.

DIGITAL RHETORICS

The Digital Rhetorics Syllabus Approach aims to situate students within digital discourses while they investigate the applications of digital spaces in their classes, their work, and their lives. If we see and understand these digital spaces and the information, connections, and productions contained within as inexorable from the real world, then students must become literate within these spaces or risk lacking the tools to work and compose effectively. These concerns will shape the entirety of the course, while also directing the students' writing, reading, and projects. While the course is grounded within textual composition, writing concerns, and rhetorical appeals, students will also focus on questions of access, literacy, play/invention, genre/medium, and fair use/ownership. These questions will apply both to the students themselves and their audiences as they work with digital rhetorics on and offline, with new technology, and with digital spaces such as sites, forums, wikis, blogs, and YouTube.

During the course, we establish digital rhetorics as an umbrella term for the way in which we interact with information today. This course does not aim to study digital rhetorics as a type of cultural studies separate from ourselves, but instead as the very grounding of our ability to find, interpret, and use information in the digital age. With more and more information being stored and created digitally, students need to develop a research literacy that will help them not only understand these issues, but overcome and utilize them as well. This does not mean simply covering these concepts during class lectures, but rather putting these ideas into practice.

STUDENTS CRITIQUE THE VARIOUS METHODS THAT SOCIETY USES TO DOCUMENT AND PRESENT THE WORLD

DOCUMENTING REALTIES

Documenting Realities asks students to engage, analyze and explore the ways in which the world around them is documented. This syllabus approach asks students to critique the various methods that society uses to document and present the world, and participate in the process as they document their own realities. Students analyze familiar methods of documentation, including web, print, and video media websites, television, newspapers, and magazines, from a critical and rhetorically informed perspective. They are also challenged to consider the effectiveness of less obvious media that purport to document reality, such as art, film, and music. Using a genre approach to writing, this syllabus asks students to adapt their writing to a variety of rhetorical situations and audiences, allowing them to better understand the multifaceted purposes to which writing can be directed.

While this approach allows for both the analysis and creation of various documentary methods and media, instructors have the freedom to focus upon methods and media that interest them or lie within their area of expertise. Instructors also have the option of choosing one overarching theme for the entire course, such as an environmental, ethnographic or multicultural approach. Frequently courses focus on an exploration of current local, national and/or international events of importance. Students learn to cultivate their critical thinking skills through a variety of assignments and class discussion topics.

UR@

UR@ sees the act of composition as a process of locating oneself within and engaging with interdisciplinary discourses in order to move through networks of relations within and across spaces. In short, this approach encourages students to locate themselves in relation to contemporary cultural domains and engage with various media, such as film, music, text, and webtext. While incorporating aspects of traditional composition instruction, this approach also provides space for play, which enables movement and flow, invention and discovery, all necessary components of creative composition. In addition, UR@ acknowledges that the shifting landscape of technology requires an agile and sophisticated command of new compositional strategies.

In UR@, students explore the interconnectedness of contemporary literacies, stretch this interconnectedness through play, and write in as many genres and media as possible: students understand (read and interpret), play (investigate and experiment), and then compose (write and design). The ways in which particular instructors enact this third element and the ways in which students play emphasize UR@'s flexibility and dynamism.

WRITING ABOUT WRITING

In this approach, you'll find yourself learning and writing *about* writing. You'll read research on the ways that writing works and do your own investigations, too. You'll become a developing expert on how writing works in various communities including your own academic field or discipline. Although Writing About Writing courses can be taught in a variety of ways, this approach, as taught by instructors at Purdue, typically includes the following units: Literacies, Rhetorical Situations, Discourse Communities, and Academic or Disciplinary Discourse. If you have no idea what these terms mean, don't worry. By the end of your Writing About Writing course, you'll be using them like a pro!

If you're in a Writing About Writing course, you'll see that this approach:

1) Believes that you learn something about a topic when you read and write about it. That's why this course asks you to read about writing and write about writing. If you're going to be in a writing course for a whole semester, why not learn the most you can about how to write!

2) Positions you, the student, as an expert. By drawing on your past experiences and high-lighting literacies outside the university, the approach values the experiences and expertise of all course participants. You might know a whole lot more than your teacher about some kinds of writing—maybe you know more about about html coding or blogging—but your teacher also brings his or her expertise, too.

3) Offers you the opportunity to find out straight from the source what researchers have learned about writing. You'll get to read the articles that usually only teachers read in order to see for yourself what we know about how students and professionals *really* write at the university and beyond.

WRITING YOUR WAY INTO PURDUE

Originating out of interests in social action, the course is often currently structured around student issues of identity and community and therefore well-positioned to take advantage of their daily interactions with the institutional University community, the local West Lafayette community and the multiple global identities and communities inhabiting the West Lafayette Campus. This approach encourages the instructor to access the wealth of material on campus and in its environs in generating thoughtful and broadening writing and living experiences for their composition students. Instructors are encouraged to incorporate the wide variety of cultural productions on campus, from Purdue Theater to Convocations, and the various art gallery spaces in the Purdue Union, Stewart Center, or Pao Visual and Performing Arts Building into their writing assignments. University-affiliated organizations such as the Black Cultural Center, the Native American Cultural Center, and the International Center, and the large number of student organizations are all rich sources of material for composition assignments.

Textbooks Used by Introductory Courses

All ICaP courses use a textbook or coursepack that has been approved by the ICaP program. In addition to one of the textbooks listed below or an approved coursepack, your course may be supplemented by additional readings. All English 10600-I sections use a common coursepack.

Textbooks used in English 10600 and English 10600-R are listed in the following chart:

Approved for:	Textbook Title, Author(s), Publisher
ALL Syllabus Approaches	*Academic Research and Writing* by Bergmann. Longman. *Compose, Design, Advocate* by Wysocki and Lynch. Longman. *The Norton Field Guide to Writing* by Bullock. Norton. *Writing: A Manual for a Digital Age* by Blakesley. Wadsworth. *Writing Today* by Johnson-Sheehan and Paine. Pearson.
Academic Writing and Research	*A Short Guide to College Writing* by Barnet, Bellanca and Stubbs. Longman. *Everything's an Argument* by Lunsford and Ruszkiewicz. Bedford/St. Martin's. *From Inquiry to Academic Writing* by Greene and Lidinsky. Bedford/St.Martin's.
Composing Through Literature	*Literature for Composition: Interactive Edition*, 8th ed. by Barnet, Burto, and Cain. Longman. *Responding to Literature*, 5th ed. by Stanford. McGraw-Hill. *Writing about Literature* by Gardner. Bedford/St.Martin's.
Composing With Popular Culture	*Acting Out Culture: Reading and Writing* by James Miller. Bedford/St.Martin's. *Beyond Words: Cultural Texts for Reading and Writing* by Ruszkiewicz, Anderson, and Friend. Longman. *Dynamics in Document Design: Creating Text for Readers* by Karen Schriver. Wiley. *Envision* by Alfano and O'Brien. Longman. *Rhetorical Visions: Reading and Writing in a Visual Culture* by Hesford and Bruggeman. Pearson.

Approved for:	Textbook Title, Author(s), Publisher
Documenting Realities	*Beyond Words: Cultural Texts for Reading and Writing* by Ruszkiewicz, Anderson, and Friend. Longman *Everything's an Argument* by Lunsford and Ruszkiewicz. Bedford/St. Martin's. *Humble Argument* by Roy K. Humble. Problem Child Press. *Inventing Arguments* by John Mauk and John Metz. Wadsworth. *The Call to Write* by John Trimbur. Longman.
Digital Rhetorics	*Joining the Conversation: Writing in College and Beyond* by Mike Palmquist. Bedford/St. Martin's. *Writing Now: Shaping Words and Images* by Lee Odell. Bedford/St. Martin's. *Write Now* by Daniel Anderson. Pearson.
UR@	*Convergences: Themes, Texts, and Images for Composition* by Atwan. Bedford/St. Martin's. *Picturing Texts* by Cynthia Selfe. Norton. *The World is a Text: Writing, Reading and Thinking About Visual and Popular Culture*, 3rd ed. by Silverman. Prentice Hall.
Writing About Writing	*Writing About Writing: A College Reader* by Elizabeth Wardle and Doug Downs. Bedford/St.Martin's.
Writing Your Way Into Purdue	*Envision* by Alfano and O'Brien. Longman. *The Concise McGraw-Hill Guide* by Roen, Glau, and Maid. McGraw-Hill. *Write Now* by Anderson. Prentice Hall.

English 10800 sections use a common coursepack that includes the readings listed. Additionally, instructors choose another textbook that corresponds with the kinds of writing that students will be doing in their 10800 course. This additional textbook can be selected from the books approved for any of the 10600 approaches.

	ICaP 10800 Coursepack
All sections of English 10800	"What does it mean to be a citizen?" by Berdt and Muse (Chapter 1 from *Composing a Civic Life*)
	"A New Era of Service" by President Barack Obama
	"Service Learning as a Path to Virtue" by Jim Dubinsky
	"Rhetorician as Agent of Social Change" by Ellen Cushman
	"Preparing for Outreach: Respect and Reciprocity" (from *Writing and Community Action*) by Thomas Deans
	"Race, Class, and Whiteness" by Ann Green
	"Knowledgework with the Cherokee Nation" by Ellen Cushman and Green (From *The Public Work of Rhetoric*)

2

What Can I Expect from My ICaP Course?

Expect Something Different than High School

Grading and Commenting: What kinds of feedback can I expect to receive?

Participation: What will be expected of me?

Top Ten Excuses that Just Won't Work

The Workload: What kinds of work can I expect to do in ICaP courses?

Top Ten Reasons to Take and Enjoy Your Composition Course

THE GOAL: BY THE END OF THIS CHAPTER, YOU'LL KNOW WHAT TO EXPECT FROM YOUR ICaP COURSE AND WHAT YOUR INSTRUCTOR AND THE ICaP PROGRAM WILL EXPECT OF YOU IN TERMS OF CLASS PREPARATION AND PARTICIPATION.

What Can I Expect From My ICaP Course?

In this chapter you'll find out just what to expect from your ICaP course, and you'll also see what's going to be expected of *you*. ICaP courses, as you know, are geared toward meeting a set of goals that involve more than just producing polished texts: they involve developing a composing process and becoming a critical thinker, reader, and writer. These process-oriented goals make ICaP courses seem a little different, so your course will probably be different than the classes you took in high school and different than the "traditional" English course in your head. Yes, that's right, this is not your mama's composition class.

THIS IS NOT YOUR MAMA'S COMPOSITION CLASS

Expect Something Different from High School

If you're trying to compare your ICaP class to that English class you took in high school, you should stop that right now. Expect things to be a little different. The tables that follow will help adjust your expectations for your ICaP course and maybe for your college courses in general.

How Is College Different From High School? | 1

Following the Rules in High School	Choosing Responsibly in College
High school is mandatory and usually free.	College is voluntary and expensive.
Your time is structured by others.	You manage your own time.
You need permission to participate in extra-curricular activities.	You must decide whether to participate in co-curricular activities.
You can count on parents and teachers to remind you of your responsibilities and guide you in setting priorities.	You must balance your responsibilities and set priorities. You will face moral and ethical decisions you have never faced before.
Each day you proceed from one class directly to another, spending 6 hours each day—30 hours a week—in class.	You often have hours between classes; class times vary throughout the day and evening and you spend only 12 to 16 hours each week in class.
Most of your classes are arranged for you.	You arrange your own schedule in consultation with your adviser. Schedules tend to look lighter than they really are.
You are not responsible for knowing what it takes to graduate.	Graduation requirements are complex, and differ from year to year. You are expected to know those that apply to you.
Guiding principle: You will usually be told what to do and corrected if your behavior is out of line.	**Guiding principle:** You are expected to take responsibility for what you do and don't do, as well as for the consequences of your decisions.

Tables used with permission from the Altshuler Learning Enhancement Center at Southern Methodist University <http://smu.edu/alec/tranisition.asp>.

YOU MUST BALANCE YOUR RESPONSIBILITIES AND SET PRIORITIES.

How Is College Different From High School? `2`

GOING TO HIGH SCHOOL CLASSES	SUCCEEDING IN COLLEGE CLASSES
The school year is 36 weeks long; some classes extend over both semesters and some don't.	The academic year is divided into two separate 15-week semesters, plus a week after each semester for exams.
Classes generally have no more than 35 students.	Classes may number 100 students or more.
You may study outside class as little as 0 to 2 hours a week, and this may be mostly last-minute test preparation.	You need to study at least 2 to 3 hours outside of class for each hour in class.
You seldom need to read anything more than once, and sometimes listening in class is enough.	You need to review class notes and text material regularly.
You are expected to read short assignments that are then discussed, and often re-taught, in class.	You are assigned substantial amounts of reading and writing which may not be directly addressed in class.
Guiding principle: You will usually be told in class what you need to learn from assigned reading.	**Guiding principle:** College is a learning environment in which you take responsibility for thinking through and applying what you have learned.

**YOU TAKE RESPONSIBLITY
FOR THINKING THROUGH
AND APPLYING WHAT YOU
HAVE LEARNED.**

How Is College Different From High School? 3

HIGH SCHOOL TEACHERS	COLLEGE PROFESSORS
Teachers check your completed homework.	Professors may not always check completed homework, but they will assume you can perform the same tasks on tests.
Teachers remind you of your incomplete work.	Professors may not remind you of incomplete work.
Teachers approach you if they believe you need assistance.	Professors are usually open and helpful, but most expect you to initiate contact if you need assistance.
Teachers are often available for conversation before, during, or after class.	Professors expect and want you to attend their scheduled office hours.
Teachers have been trained in teaching methods to assist in imparting knowledge to students.	Professors have been trained as experts in their particular areas of research.
Teachers provide you with information you missed when you were absent.	Professors expect you to get from classmates any notes from classes you missed.
Teachers present material to help you understand the material in the textbook.	Professors may not follow the textbook. Instead, to amplify the text, they may give illustrations, provide background information, or discuss research about the topic you are studying. Or they may expect you to relate the classes to the textbook readings.
Teachers often write information on the board to be copied in your notes.	Professors may lecture nonstop, expecting you to identify the important points in your notes. When professors write on the board, it may be to amplify the lecture, not to summarize it. Good notes are a must.
Teachers impart knowledge and facts, sometimes drawing direct connections and leading you through the thinking process.	Professors expect you to think about and synthesize seemingly unrelated topics.
Teachers often take time to remind you of assignments and due dates.	Professors expect you to read, save, and consult the course syllabus (outline); the syllabus spells out exactly what is expected of you, when it is due, and how you will be graded.

How Is College Different From High School?   *cont.*

HIGH SCHOOL TEACHERS	COLLEGE PROFESSORS
Teachers carefully monitor class attendance.	Professors may not formally take roll, but they are still likely to know whether or not you attended.
Guiding principle: High school is a teaching environment in which you acquire facts and skills.	**Guiding principle:** College is a learning environment in which you take responsibility for thinking through and applying what you have learned.

How Is College Different From High School?   4

TESTS IN HIGH SCHOOL	TESTS IN COLLEGE
Testing is frequent and covers small amounts of material.	Testing is usually infrequent and may be cumulative, covering large amounts of material. You, not the professor, need to organize the material to prepare for the test. A particular course may have only 2 or 3 tests in a semester.
Makeup tests are often available.	Makeup tests are seldom an option; if they are, you need to request them.
Teachers frequently rearrange test dates to avoid conflict with school events.	Professors in different courses usually schedule tests without regard to the demands of other courses or outside activities.
Teachers frequently conduct review sessions, pointing out the most important concepts.	Professors rarely offer review sessions, and when they do, they expect you to be an active participant, one who comes prepared with questions.
Guiding principle: Mastery is usually seen as the ability to reproduce what you were taught in the form in which it was presented to you, or to solve the kinds of problems you were shown how to solve.	**Guiding principle:** Mastery is often seen as the ability to apply what you've learned to new situations or to solve new kinds of problems.

How Is College Different From High School?   5

GRADES IN HIGH SCHOOL	GRADES IN COLLEGE
Grades are given for most assigned work.	Grades may not be provided for all assigned work.
Consistently good homework grades may raise your overall grade when test grades are low.	Grades on tests and major papers usually provide most of the course grade.
Extra credit projects are often available to help you raise your grade.	Grades on tests and major papers usually provide most of the course grade.
Initial test grades, especially when they are low, may not have an adverse effect on your final grade.	Watch out for your first tests. These are usually "wake-up calls" to let you know what is expected—but they also may account for a substantial part of your course grade. You may be shocked when you get your grades.
You may graduate as long as you have passed all required courses with a grade of D or higher.	You may graduate only if your average in classes meets the departmental standard—typically a 2.0 or C.
Guiding principle: Effort counts. Courses are usually structured to reward a "good-faith effort."	**Guiding principle:** Results count. Though "good-faith effort" is important in regard to the professor's willingness to help you achieve good results, it will not substitute for results in the grading process.

"GOOD-FAITH EFFORT"... WILL NOT SUBSTITUTE FOR RESULTS IN THE GRADING PROCESS.

Grading and Commenting:
What kinds of feedback can I expect to receive?

As a student in an ICaP course, you can expect to receive feedback and grades on your assignments in a timely manner. Feedback may be delayed in extraordinary circumstances such as instructor illness or zombie apocalypse. Feedback may be given in the form of substantial written comments or in face-to-face conferencing with the instructor.

During your composing process, you can also expect to receive specific assignment guidelines and evaluation criteria. Grades on your final project drafts will be clearly marked, and you can expect to receive an explanation of why your assignment earned the grade that it did. Sometimes, your instructor may require you to come to his or her office hours to discuss your grade.

While it would be nice to have your instructor remind you of your grades via email from time to time or to share that information with curious parents, neither of these is actually possible because of FERPA (Family Educational Rights and Privacy Act) which prevents instructors from emailing or posting grades in non-secure locations such as office doors (even if they are listed by anonymizing numbers). For this reason, you can expect your grades to be shared with you only through secure, university approved means such as MyPurdue, Blackboard, or Drupal.

Participation: What will be expected of me?

Because of the social nature of the process of composing, it will be imperative that you attend and participate in the class. Our Introductory Composition courses revolve around group discussion, peer evaluation, and a number of in-class, group assignments that reinforce or clarify the work of the class. These assignments are a regular part of the class itself and may or may not appear on the syllabus or receive official letter grades. Often, the points designated for these activities are included in the generic heading "Participation." (*For more details on how this fits into the Goals of the Introductory Composition courses overall please see "Shared Goals" in the previous chapter, "What Is ICaP?"*)

DISCUSSION

During the course of the semester it is expected that you will come to class having used the books that you purchased (i.e. that you will have done the reading) and that you will be ready and willing to discuss the readings in a meaningful and respectful way. Your teacher will be excited to hear what it is that you have to say and even more excited if you can articulate why it is that you agree or disagree with what it is that you have read for class. Instructors don't necessarily assign readings because they agree with them or want you to, but rather because they want to engage you in the topic and make you think. Discussion works best if you have actually done the reading.

IN-CLASS OR GROUP ASSIGNMENTS

From time to time your instructor may assign in-class or group assignments that range from doing an impromptu debate style activity to preparing notes for a class discussion. These are learning activities, and everyone is expected to participate in them equally. These activities do affect not only your grade in the class ("Participation"), but also help you to become a better composer/writer. These assignments often cannot be "made up" if you miss the class that they were assigned in; therefore, regular class attendance is crucial.

PEER REVIEW

Although your instructor's feedback is important to your writing process, your peers' feedback is also crucial. Throughout the semester, your instructor will integrate formal peer review sessions in class or out of class in order to give you the opportunity to give and receive feedback during the writing process. Peer review is your opportunity (1) to have another set of eyes (besides the teacher's) on your writing before it is turned in as a final draft and (2) to participate in a personalized and colloquial discussion about your and your classmates' work. Peer review is a workshop geared toward improvement and development of key elements in the project. On the one hand, it is not a "feel better" session for your classmates. On the other hand, this is not a time to transform into Captain "Correct-This" or Dr. "Doing-It-Wrong" and tell a peer that his or her work is "bad." Instead, you are to carefully read and consider the work of your peers with the intention of offering constructive, advice-centered comments that pair intuitive questions with productive suggestions. Read your peers' work carefully, with the intention of giving them the best advice, suggestions, and feedback possible.

READ YOUR PEERS' WORK CAREFULLY, WITH THE INTENTION OF GIVING THEM THE BEST ADVICE, SUGGESTIONS, AND FEEDBACK POSSIBLE.

Top Ten Excuses (that Just Won't Work) for Missing Class or Not Turning in Assignments

1. **I overslept.**
   Alarm clock? Earlier bedtime? Later class? Rig a bucket of ice water to your alarm?

2. **My computer died / I saved it to the wrong disk / my file won't open / the dog ate my homework.**
   The strangest things seem to happen to homework assignments and essays so it is always a good idea to save frequently, print a copy, save a copy to external media (like a key drive), and save a copy to your career account H drive. Oh yes, and make sure you double check to make sure that it is actually there before you log off of the computer.

3. **I was sick...so sick I couldn't even email.**
   We're so glad that you are feeling well enough to rejoin the class and that you are no longer contagious...you're not, right? It's always a good idea to bring a detailed physician's note to school with you when you return. The class absence policy is on the syllabus and if you need special consideration please feel free to contact the Dean of Students' Office for medical withdrawal or extended absence information.

4. **There was a family emergency/death in the family.**
   We're sorry for your loss and you have our deepest condolences, but the university has a standard policy for absence following the death of a family member.

5. **I didn't get the assignment / I didn't know the due date / I didn't understand what we were supposed to do.**
   All assignments and due dates are listed on the syllabus. If you have lost your original copy it is always available online at the course website. If all else fails you can always call upon your instructor or classmates for a little assistance.

6. **I was studying for another class.**
   Uh huh.

7. **I forgot what day I had class/conferences. I forgot which room we were in.**
   Please refer to the handy calendar in the front of this book. Remember, the one you filled out at the beginning of the semester? Yes, that one.

8. **I dropped my key down the elevator shaft. I got locked out of my car / dorm room / apartment.**
   A little notification goes a long way. If some such misfortune befalls you, just take a second (while waiting for maintenance or the locksmith) to give your instructor a call or send her an email. If you have something due you can also submit it electronically so as not to have it be too terribly late.

9. **My roommate is having a really difficult time right now.**
   There are many resources available on campus to help students who are struggling with a variety of issues. See the resources section of this book and refer your roommate to them. By the way, none of the urban legends about roommates and the mythical "all A semester" are actually true.

10. **I couldn't do the homework because I don't have my book yet.**
    In the rare case where the book is out of stock or you just haven't been able to buy it yet, it is still your responsibility to keep up with the readings in your courses. You can borrow a book from a classmate and copy it, talk to the instructor, see if the library has a copy. Falling behind in the reading at the beginning of the semester never works out well in the end.

The Workload:
What kinds of work can I expect to do in ICaP courses?

COMPOSING THROUGH VARIOUS GENRES AND MEDIA

You will be expected to compose in various genres and with various media in this course. This may include writing letters to the editor, review essays, and research papers. You may also be asked to analyze non-alphanumeric or non-print based texts such as films, video games, or photo essays. Please keep in mind that these analyses are all done rhetorically and hold as much intellectual merit as their more traditional counterparts.

In addition to writing more traditional alphanumeric texts (i.e. essays, reviews, and letters) in your Introductory Composition course, your instructor will assign at least one multimodal assignment as well that can include web page building, audio recording & editing, or video recording & editing. Don't worry if you don't know how to do these things at the beginning of the class: your instructor will provide adequate resources for you to work though these things, and you will not be expected to work at a level that exceeds your ability.

CONFERENCING

Regular conferences will be invaluable to you in your ICaP course. If you're taking English 10600, you will conference one-on-one with your instructor each week or at least every other week during your assigned course conferencing time to discuss your assignments or progress in the course. (You may conference more often if you set up appointments during office hours.) If you're taking English 10800, you can set up one-on-one conferences during your instructor's designated office hours. Coming to conferences prepared to talk about your writing makes conferencing even more productive. Using the pre-conference form at the end of this book is highly recommended as is using the post-conferencing form to reflect upon the conference afterwards. (*For more on conferencing and attendance please see the specific sections in the "Policies" section of this book*).

RESEARCH

Another thing that you can expect to do in your ICaP course is research. Because research at the college level involves not just reading and synthesizing material but also contributing new, original ideas to a larger conversation, ICaP courses will often integrate both primary and secondary research. Most ICaP students are very familiar with secondary research, but few have conducted primary research in which they gather new data to learn about a topic or issue. Even if you haven't conducted primary research before, you can expect to learn about some of the ways that this kind of research can be conducted and why it's important in particular fields or projects. (*For more information about primary and secondary research and the expectations for citing sources of information, see "What Should I Know about Research and Writing?"*)

In your ICaP course, you can expect to compose in new ways, participate in the process of collaborative learning, and develop your writing abilities, and you can also expect a few perks along the way. Here are at least ten reasons that you should take (and enjoy) your course!

Top Ten Reasons to Take (and Enjoy) Your Composition Course

1. **You'll have a small class size.**
   You will have no more than 19 classmates in your composition class. You'll get to know them (and their writing) quite well. Instant friends!

2. **Your instructor will know your name.**
   With only 20 students in the class, your instructor will know your name. You will be something other than your PUID number, and your instructor will have office hours if you'd like to talk about your work outside of class.

3. **Writing in college is not the same as writing in high school.**
   Whether you wrote a lot or a little in your previous courses, you'll find that writing in upper level college courses and writing outside the university requires you to adapt to new rhetorical situations, compose in new genres, integrate multiple media, etc.— and these are just the things that ICaP courses emphasize. (Don't worry, if the term "rhetorical situation" doesn't sound familiar yet, your ICaP course is the right place for you!)

4. **If you are already a good writer, your composition course could be a GPA boost!**
   Even if you did well in high school composition (yeah!), you need to continue to write to hone your skills. The writing you did in high school was prep work for what you'll do now.

5. **You'll get to practice, practice, practice!**
   Do you play soccer? Knit? Play guitar? You have to practice to improve your skills, right? The same is true for writing, and your composition course gives you the opportunity to practice and improve your skills with instruction.

6. **Your composition instructor is a pretty good resource.**
   Need a letter of recommendation for Study Abroad? Can't figure out how to organize your paper for history class? Need a job and don't have a résumé? Need to know where the best ice cream in town is sold? Ask your instructor. If she can't help you, she can direct you to someone who can.

7. **You'll learn about composition in a whole new way.**
   You'll learn to produce a variety of texts—films, books, comics, games, articles, websites. In the process, you'll also learn how to analyze these texts in rhetorically sound ways and to think about how they operate in a larger social context.

8. **You'll learn about the Libraries (notice that "Library" is plural) at Purdue.**
   You might take a field trip to visit one or more of the libraries. You might learn about information retrieval, "The Stacks," or archives. Also, there's a nifty coffee shop outside of Hicks Undergraduate Library.

9. **You'll take your writing skills with you.**
   You'll learn to write for different audiences, in different genres, with different media. Whatever you learn, you'll be able to transfer it to your major or field. But remember: you have to practice your skills to keep and improve them.

10. **You'll use and improve your technology skills.**
    Not all compositions are written on 8 ½" x 11" paper. You might use your composing skills to create a web page, a podcast, a brochure, a short video, or a poster. You may learn to use software you've never tried before. Either way, you'll learn about visual rhetoric and how visuals impact your communication.

WHATEVER YOU LEARN, YOU'LL BE ABLE TO TRANSFER IT TO YOUR MAJOR OR FIELD.

3

What Resources Are Available to Me?

Your Instructor

Introductory Composition at Purdue (ICaP) Office

English Department Office

Purdue Writing Lab

Digital Learning Collaboratory (DLC)

Counseling Services

Sexual Harassment Advisor's Network (SHAN)

THE GOAL: BY THE END OF THIS CHAPTER, YOU'LL KNOW HOW TO CONTACT YOUR INSTRUCTOR AND HOW TO FIND OUT IF A CLASS SESSION HAS BEEN CANCELLED. YOU'LL KNOW HOW THE WRITING LAB CAN BENEFIT YOU IF YOU WANT TO WORK ON YOUR WRITING OUTSIDE YOUR SCHEDULED CLASS TIMES. YOU'LL ALSO BE ABLE TO IDENTIFY A FEW OF THE MANY PURDUE ACRONYMS: CAPS, DLC, DOS, ORC, SAO, SHAN, AND MAYBE A FEW MORE, TOO!

What Resources Are Available to Me?

One of the best resources you have at Purdue is your composition instructor. You are in a class of twenty (or fewer) students, so you can expect your instructor to know your name and learn a lot about you during the semester. Your instructor will have one hour a week set aside for drop-in office hours, but your instructor will also be available other times for student appointments. Office hour times will be posted on your instructor's office door and printed on the course syllabus.

Your Course Instructor

ICaP instructors do not have office phones, so most likely outside of class you will communicate with your instructor via email. If you do not have your instructor's email written down, you may look it up on the Purdue Directory at http://www.itap.purdue.edu/directory. Any other contact information your instructor wants you to use will be available on your course syllabus.

Introductory Composition at Purdue (ICaP) Office

Heavilon Hall, Room 302
(765) 494-3730
http://www.digitalparlor.org/icap
Secretary: Joy Kane

If you have a question about your composition class or you are having a conflict with your instructor, please see Joy Kane, the secretary of ICaP. She can direct you to speak with the appropriate person.

If your instructor does not show up 10 minutes after class has commenced, you should first check your email or the course website (on a smartphone or the computer available in the classroom) to see if your instructor has left a cancellation message. If nothing shows up there, call or visit the ICaP office (494-3730, HEAV 302) and ask if the instructor has cancelled class.

If your instructor repeatedly cancels class or does not show up, please contact the ICaP office.

English Department Office

Heavilon Hall, Room 324
(765) 494-3740
http://www.cla.purdue.edu/english

You may need to visit the English Department main office if the ICaP office is closed. The main office is also where you might find lost & found items.

Purdue Writing Lab

Heavilon Hall, Room 226

(765) 494-3723

http://owl.english.purdue.edu

The Writing Lab offers many free services to students, faculty, and staff. Central to the Writing Lab's services are one-on-one tutorials for students at any stage in their writing process. Tutors can offer you a second reader's response to a draft, help to see if you understand an assignment, answer questions you might have, review grammar rules you might need, help you with planning or revising your paper, assist with learning how to search the Web for information for papers, or work with you on other writing concerns. Writing Lab staff will not 1) offer an evaluation of your paper or a possible grade or 2) proofread your paper.

The tutors are ready to help you learn how to proofread or to help you see what categories of error to proofread for, but they will not go over your paper and correct the errors for you. The core of a tutorial is talk—conversations about ideas you might have for a paper, dialogue that leads you to answer your own questions, and talk that helps you refine your ideas and ask the questions you have about a draft of a paper or an assignment.

> FOR A PRODUCTIVE SESSION WITH YOUR WRITING LAB TUTOR, BRING SOMETHING YOU'VE WRITTEN, BRING YOUR ASSIGNMENT SHEET, AND BRING SOME QUESTIONS/TOPICS YOU WANT TO ADDRESS.

You may come to the Writing Lab at any time in your writing process. Your tutorial will be more effective if you bring something you've written and your assignment sheet, and if you have a clear idea of what you want to work on. Your instructor may recommend that you see a tutor and perhaps offer you some guidance on areas of your writing in which a tutoring session might help. However, if you have no paper, no assignment, and no idea of what you want to work on other than a vague wish to improve your writing, it is hard to accomplish anything worthwhile.

The Writing Lab offers consultations 9:00AM–6:00PM on Monday through Thursday, and 9:00AM–1:00PM on Friday. You can call 494-3723 to make an appointment, or try to make a same-day drop-in reservation after 9AM. Writing consultations are also available in the HSSE Library on Mondays from 7:00–10:00PM, in Meredith Hall on Wednesdays from 7:00–10:00PM, and in the Latino Cultural Center on Tuesdays from 6:00–9:00PM. For more information and the most up-to-date schedules, please call 494-3723 or visit http://owl.english.purdue.edu. Whenever you visit the Writing Lab, be sure to bring your student ID.

The Writing Lab offers the following services in addition to tutorials:

- **OWL (Online Writing Lab)**

    This website has over 100 handouts on writing skills that you can refer to or download. There are also online workshops on writing research papers and writing resumes, podcasts that offer additional information on the writing process, a YouTube channel that hosts lots of videos on different elements of the research and writing process, plus suggestions for how to search the web effectively, and links to useful references and the most commonly used search engines. Visit the OWL at http://owl.english.purdue.edu. The OWL mail feature allows anyone to submit questions about writing. The OWL also provides a direct link to OpenStudy, a website for students to ask and answer questions.

- **Computers for Student Use**

  All of the computers in the Writing Lab are connected to the Internet, and while some are reserved for tutorial use, others are available (when not being used for tutorials) for student use.

- **Study/Writing Area**

  When there are unoccupied tutoring tables, students are invited to use that space for writing or studying, and they are invited to use any of our reference materials and to ask questions about writing.

- **ESL Conversation Groups**

  If your first language is not English, you may join an ESL Conversation Group, hosted by The Writing Lab. At the conversation group you'll meet new people, learn more about different cultures, and discuss topics of interest to you and to the group. A Writing Lab consultant will assist the group with vocabulary or expressions you may not know. You do not need to make an appointment to join a conversation group; drop-in times are posted on the Writing Lab website at http://owl.english.purdue.edu/writinglab/esl.

Writing Lab staff can:	Writing Lab staff will not:
Offer you a second reader's response to a draft	Offer an evaluation of your paper
Help you see if you understand an assignment	Tell you what they think your grade will be
Review grammar rules you might not know or remember	Proofread your paper for you
Help you with planning or revising your paper	Do the work for you
Assist with learning how to search the Web for information for papers	
Work with you on other writing projects (outside your ICaP course)	

Digital Learning Collaboratory (DLC)

Hicks Undergraduate Library, Room B853

http://www.dlc.purdue.edu

The DLC's mission "is to support and facilitate integrated learning of information and technology literacy for Purdue University students." You may use the DLC's collaboration rooms, computer labs, and workstations equipped with high-end audio and video software. You may also check out audio/visual and computer equipment for class projects.

Counseling Services

Counseling and Psychological Services (CAPS)

Student Health Center

601 Stadium Mall Drive, Room 246

(765) 494-6995

http://www.purdue.edu/caps

CAPS works with Purdue students, staff, and faculty to provide individual counseling, group counseling, crisis prevention, drug and alcohol consultation, psychological testing, and psychiatric services. CAPS is located in the Student Health Center and in the Psychological Sciences Building (PSYC).

Purdue Counseling and Guidance Center

100 North University Street

Beering Hall, Room 3202

(765) 494-9738

http://www.edst.purdue.edu/counseling_psychology/PCGC.html

The Counseling and Guidance Center is available for "those whose concerns and problems are not of a magnitude that prevents them from meeting daily responsibilities and those who are not in crisis. We provide no psychiatric or medical service, nor can we serve those individuals with severe psychological disorders."

Lafayette Crisis Center

1244 North 15th Street

Lafayette, IN 47904-2114

Crisis Line: (765) 742-0244

Toll Free: (877) 419-1632

Call the Lafayette Crisis Center for 24-hour crisis intervention, information, referrals, suicide prevention, and rape advocacy.

Dean of Students

Schleman Hall

http://www.purdue.edu/odos/

The DOS, a department of the Division of Student Affairs, includes many offices that serve different parts of the Purdue student body. The main Dean of Students offices you might encounter include Counseling, Student Rights and Responsibilities (OSRR), Student Activities & Organizations (SAO), Disability Resource Center (DRC), and Horizons.

Sexual Harassment Advisors Network (SHAN)

The Sexual Harassment Advisors Network offers support, help, and advice for students who believe they may be victims of sexual harassment. Advisors in SHAN will help you explore your options whether or not you wish to pursue action. See http://www.cla.purdue.edu/resources/shan for more information.

What Software and New Technologies Will I Need to Use / Learn?

THE GOAL: BY THE END OF THIS CHAPTER, YOU'LL KNOW WHAT KIND OF STORAGE SPACE AND SOFTWARE PURDUE PROVIDES FOR YOU, HOW TO ACCESS YOUR HOME DIRECTORY (H DRIVE), AND HOW TO COMPOSE AN APPROPRIATE E-MAIL TO YOUR INSTRUCTOR. THESE AND THE OTHER TECHNOLOGY RESOURCES MENTIONED IN THIS CHAPTER WILL HELP YOU AS YOU COMPLETE YOUR DAY-TO-DAY ACTIVITIES AND YOUR WRITING PROJECTS.

What Software and New Technologies Will I Need to Use / Learn?

In your ICaP writing courses you will find that you will be using some basic computer skills in your day-to-day work. These will include email, attaching files, and word processing. While your instructor can work with you on these things, some basic familiarity will be helpful.

What Software Will I Need to Use / Learn?

As the course goes on you may be asked to interact with some more advanced software programs such as presentation software, image editing, and audio editing programs. Your instructor will provide you with adequate instruction and/or resources to learn these various technologies.

All of the software that you are asked to use in class will be standard on all of the computers in the Purdue computer labs. It should also be noted that Purdue provides you with both discounts on versions of much of this software and free remote access to many of the same software suites that are available on the computer lab machines. In the rare case where a program is not provided by the university it will be listed on the syllabus/booklist as a required text and should be purchased by you as such.

If your instructor requires you to email or upload documents to a particular person or online storage space, she will provide you with specific email addresses or URLs as well as specifying which file format is required. You are expected to comply with these reasonable requests.

Your instructor may ask you to name your individual files and file folders in a specific way in order to make sure that the files are easily navigable for evaluation. Your ICaP instructor will go over these naming protocol in class and provide you with documentation so that the process is clear.

Remember:

- Your instructor will provide you with adequate instruction and/or resources to learn the various technologies required by your course.

- In the rare case where a program is not provided by the university it will be listed on the syllabus/booklist as a required text and should be purchased by you as such.

- Your instructor may ask you to name your individual files and file folders in a specific way in order to make sure that the files are easily navigable for evaluation.

What Technology Resources Are Available to Me?

Purdue provides you with 500 megabytes of virtual storage in your Purdue career account as long as you are affiliated with Purdue. By using your home directory storage space in your career account you can make carrying disks, key drives, etc. unnecessary. The home directory is always available, anytime, anywhere (you simply need to log in to the virtual drive from a computer and use it as you would any hard drive). A personal web page is also available to you (located in the "www" folder in the home directory).

TO ACCESS YOUR HOME DIRECTORY

From an ITaP lab:

- From a Windows PC, go to Windows Explorer and look for drive H:

- From an Apple Mac, your career account home directory is mounted as your home directory.

- From a Sun workstation, your career account home directory is available as an icon on the desktop.

From your personal desktop or laptop:

From your personal Windows desktop or laptop, you can access your home directory using any secure File Transfer Protocol (FTP) program or set up a Virtual Private Network (VPN) connection.

Using FTP

To use FTP, you will need a secure file transfer program.

- SecureFX is used in the ITaP PC labs and is available for free download at http://www.purdue.edu/securePurdue/download/

- Fetch is used in the ITaP Mac labs and is available for free download at http://www.fetchsoftworks.com

- Fetch is free to all Purdue staff and students by going to the "Education" section of the Fetch Softworks web page.

Use *ftp.ics.purdue.edu* for the server name and log in with your Purdue career account login and password. Any secure file transfer client can be used and many are available for free by downloading from the Internet.

Using VPN

The most secure way to access your personal storage space, Web pages, or to send documents to a campus printer from an off-campus location, is to set up a VPN connection. By using Purdue's VPN service, you can access resources that are only available on-campus, from anywhere. You can map your home directory to a drive on your own computer, print to a campus printer, or access course materials you might not otherwise be able to access from home. You don't necessarily have to be at home either; Purdue's VPN service can be accessed from anywhere in the world, any time of day or night. For more information and instructions on how to set up a VPN connection, visit http://www.itap.purdue.edu/connections/vpn/

MAPPING YOUR HOME DIRECTORY

Once you have established a VPN connection, you will need to map your Home directory to a local drive on your desktop or laptop.

If you are on-campus (in a Residence Hall, using Purdue Airlink), use the server name *rosetta.ics.purdue.edu*.

If using Windows:	\\rosetta.ics.purdue.edu\"login"
If using Macintosh:	smb://rosetta.ics.purdue.edu

If you are off-campus, use the server name *offcampus.ics.purdue.edu*.

If using Windows:	\\offcampus.ics.purdue.edu\"login"
If using Macintosh:	smb://offcampus.ics.purdue.edu

Substitute your career account login for "login."

UNIX ACCESS

UNIX can also be used to access your home directory. Your career account login and password can be used to log in to *expert.ics.purdue.edu* using a program that supports Secure Shell (SSH), giving you access to a variety of tools, including the ability to access your MySQL database account.

You may also be expected to use a course website that can be used to access your syllabus, assignments, and other documents as well as to submit assignments. The two most commonly used systems in the English department are Blackboard (which is widely used at the university) and a specially designed distribution of the Drupal CMS (Content Management System) that has developed over several years of work by specialists in the Writing Programs and focuses more clearly on the features that are needed for college level writing courses. Course site selection is at the discretion of each individual instructor. Regardless of instructor choice, all students can expect to have access to their ICaP course syllabi online.

Email: Communicating Professionally with Your Instructor

To effectively communicate with your instructor, you need to compose a professional email that includes a clear subject line, an appropriate greeting, information with the needed context or a call to action, a polite closing, and your contact information. Understanding how to write a proper email is one step toward your professionalization as a student, and later, as an employee. You need to become accustomed to writing well in all communication modes to present yourself professionally.

When composing an email, first consider your audience. Is this message going to only one person? Is it being cc'd to other people? If you are replying to an email, are you replying to only one person, or are you "Replying to All"? If you Reply to All, do you know the others on the reply list? Do they have the necessary context to understand your response? Are you saying something that you don't want someone on the reply list to read? It's important that you know who else might read your email before you click the Send button.

Subject Line: Your email requires a compact but meaningful subject line that suggests the email's content. You don't want your subject line to be twenty words long; the last part of it will not be visible in most email interfaces. But you don't want your subject line to be too short to be meaningful, either.

Greeting: Next, begin your email with a proper greeting and use a name that's appropriate for the relationship you have with the recipient. For example, if you are sending an email to an instructor you've never met, you might use the greeting, "Dear Professor Blackmon." Once you get to know your instructor, use the name he has asked you to use. If you get into the habit of including a greeting at the beginning of your emails, you'll stand out as a serious student.

Information/Call to Action: Emails are typically short documents, yet you need to provide any context your recipient needs to understand your message. Is your email merely informative? If you are going to miss class, does your email say when you will miss, why, and how you plan on making up the work? Is your email asking your recipient to do something? Is it clear what you want your reader to do?

> **TO EFFECTIVELY COMMUNICATE WITH YOUR INSTRUCTOR, YOU NEED TO COMPOSE A PROFESSIONAL EMAIL THAT INCLUDES A CLEAR SUBJECT LINE, AN APPROPRIATE GREETING, INFORMATION WITH THE NEEDED CONTEXT OR A CALL TO ACTION, A POLITE CLOSING, AND YOUR CONTACT INFORMATION.**

Closing: Many people don't give the closing of an email any thought, but the closing is important; it leaves a lasting impression with your recipients. Consider an email to your instructor in which you ask for a letter of recommendation for the Study Abroad program. If you write "Thank you for your consideration," or "My best regards," followed by your typed name, you are leaving a polite and respectful impression that could last while your instructor writes the letter for you. What is the impression your instructor might be left with if you merely say, "Thanks" or if you omit the closing? What does that say about the time you spend on the email in which you ask your instructor to spend valuable time writing for you?

Your Signature: Of course you need to "sign" your email. Your instructor can't always figure out who you are by your email address alone. You can set up your email account to include a full signature every time you send an email (if you choose), but many email programs allow you to select a signature file from several you have created.

Email as Genre: Professional email is a genre that requires a different kind of consideration from other writing. For one thing, we perceive that the transmission of our message happens instantly. The message might be sent immediately, but has it been transmitted to the reader? When you send someone an email, you cannot assume that person will be situated in the same time in which you are writing the email. You must account for the possibility that the recipient might not read the email until the following day or week. Does the recipient remember the conversation you had twenty minutes before you write your email? Maybe, if your email is read right away. The point is that you need to consider what your reader might or might not remember or know.

Grammar, Mechanics, Tone: You might equate email with texting. Please, don't. Get into the practice of giving your email more attention to detail than you do to texting. You may be used to the suggestions your cell phone makes when you misspell a word. You may also be used to texting lots of abbreviations and ignoring commas, periods, and proper grammar. That's fine when you are texting your friends, but remember with email you are not texting.

Attachments: Never email an attachment without a subject line. Many email programs will send such files to the Spam folder. Also never send an attachment with no message at all. If the recipient is not expecting an attachment from you and you don't write anything in the body of your email, your message—attachment and all—could be deleted without being read.

Let's say you are sending your instructor an electronic file of your research paper. Your subject line might be "Research Paper Submission_YourLastName" and your email might read as in E-mail 1 below. Notice the proper greeting, the message that indicates there is an attachment (and what is in that attachment), a respectful yet friendly closing, the student's name (signature) and a signature block that tells the instructor which class the student is in and offers contact information.

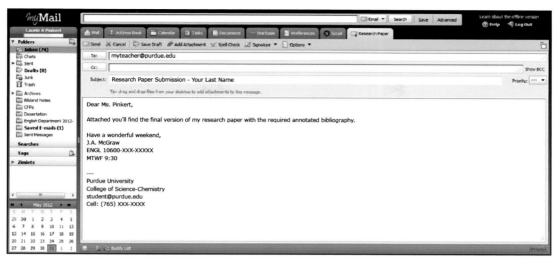

EMAIL 1: A brief and considerate email.

The following email (Email 2) doesn't offer any identifying information for the sender and is less likely to gain a response from the instructor because it doesn't ask a specific question or use a respectful tone.

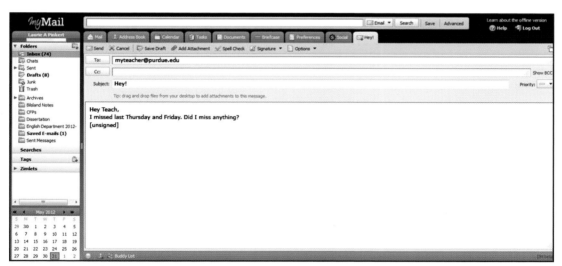

EMAIL 2: An email without a proper subject line, respectful greeting, appropriate context, or thoughtful signature.

Important Places on the Web

- **A tutorial on how to attach files to an email in MyMail:**
  http://www.digitalparlor.org/icap/node/401

- **Remote Access Computing:**
  http://www.dlc.purdue.edu

- **IT@P:**
  http://www.itap.purdue.edu

- **Student Discounts on Computer Hardware and Software:**
  http://www.itap.purdue.edu/shopping

- **DLC:**
  http://www.dlc.purdue.edu

- **Purdue Wireless Network (PAL):**
  http://www.itap.purdue.edu/airlink/index.cfm

What Should I Know
about Research and Writing?

THE GOAL: BY THE END OF THIS CHAPTER, YOU'LL KNOW THE DIFFERENCE BETWEEN PRIMARY AND SECONDARY RESEARCH AND KNOW WHAT TO CONSIDER WHEN YOU DECIDE TO DO RESEARCH FOR YOUR PROJECTS. YOU'LL ALSO KNOW A LITTLE MORE ABOUT HOW TO FIND WHAT YOU'RE LOOKING FOR AT THE PURDUE LIBRARY.

What Should I Know About Research and Writing?

No matter which ICaP course you're taking, your class will emphasize the relationship between effective writing and appropriate research. Without research, your writing projects would be one-sided, drawing only from your current knowledge or beliefs. However, with research, you can refine your own ideas about a topic and situate them in a larger conversation. Learning what kind of research you need to conduct and understanding how to effectively conduct it is crucial to your ability to develop and support your conclusions.

BECAUSE OF THE CENTRAL ROLE THAT RESEARCH PLAYS IN THE WRITING PROCESS, YOU WILL PROBABLY CONDUCT SOME KIND OF RESEARCH IN EACH OF YOUR PROJECTS; HOWEVER, YOU'LL FIND THAT DIFFERENT RHETORICAL SITUATIONS WILL REQUIRE DIFFERENT KINDS OF RESEARCH.

Because of the central role that research plays in the writing process, you will probably conduct some kind of research in each of your projects; however, you'll find that different rhetorical situations will require different kinds of research. Some situations will require that you integrate academic articles in order to explain the scholarly conversation surrounding your topic while others will require that you conduct original research on a topic that hasn't been investigated before. The type of research you conduct will depend not only on your topic but also on your intended audience. The most effective writers and researchers know how to credibly conduct and coherently integrate both primary and secondary research, the two types of research that are highlighted in the ICaP course goals.

PRIMARY RESEARCH

Primary research is research that you conduct for yourself. Common methods of primary research that are used in writing courses include interviews, surveys, and observations. This type of research can be especially useful when you are composing about a local issue. For example, if you wanted to develop a new recycling program on campus, you might need to know what percentage of students would be willing to participate in the program. Therefore, you might survey a number of students in order to see what percentage of your sample population would be willing to participate. Primary research can help you gain credibility with an audience by showing that you know how to align a research question with the appropriate research methods and that you can conduct independent, original research that will contribute to the growing body of knowledge on a topic.

For more information about conducting primary research and the things you should consider when conducting this type of research visit the Purdue OWL resource "What is Primary Research and How do I Get Started?" <http://owl.english.purdue.edu/owl/resource/559/01>.

SECONDARY RESEARCH

Secondary research is the type of research that you're probably most familiar with. This kind of research involves reading, analyzing, and synthesizing sources such as books, articles, newspapers, and magazines in order to understand what others have written or said about a given topic. Conducting secondary research can help you understand others' perspectives and can help you see the way that your position relates to those other perspectives. If you can effectively integrate secondary sources into your writing and show you understand previous research or varying opinions, you can gain credibility with your audience.

Although Google searches may sometimes yield useful results for your secondary research, you'll also need to familiarize yourself with the Purdue Libraries webpage and databases. The Libraries website not only offers access to a number of online texts but also provides a series of resources that will help you to learn how to evaluate the quality and credibility of your sources. Recently, the Purdue Libraries developed a series of online resources specifically for ICaP students; these online "LibGuides" can be found at <http://guides.lib.purdue.edu/eng106>.

Common Types of Primary Research in ICaP	Common Secondary Sources Used by ICaP Students
Surveys	Books
Interviews	Magazines
Observations	Journal articles
	Websites

Situating Your Research in the Larger Conversation

The way that you *do* research is important, and the way that you *share* your research is equally important. After all, no one will know whether or not you've done any research at all unless you share it in a way that evidences your sources of information. Whether you're sharing the interviews you conducted or your analysis of journal articles, you'll need to know how to let your audience know what kind of research you did and how it relates to the larger conversation about your topic.

Since you're taking a composition course, you'll most often be sharing your research through writing of various kinds, and you'll quickly discover that when you share your research, you need to clearly indicate which information/ideas are your own and which ones are someone else's. This clarity is important because it helps you maintain your academic honesty by ensuring that the work you present as your own is, in fact, yours; but it's also important because, by clearly explaining and citing your sources, you show how your ideas contribute to growing knowledge on a given topic. Even when you find yourself agreeing with another author or source, you still need to cite that source to show this larger conversation at work.

The way that you connect your work to a larger conversation will depend on your rhetorical situation surrounding your writing. As you know by now, the kinds of projects that you'll do in your ICaP course may vary from printed essays to digital projects to oral presentations. Because of this, the way that you cite your sources of information will vary depending on the context of the writing project. For instance, you probably won't include a list of works cited in an audio essay, but you would do so for a research paper. And if you compose blogs and websites, you'll still cite sources of information, but often through hyperlinks rather than footnotes or works cited pages.

The way you cite sources is not only dependent on the genre that you're using, it's also dependent on the audience. What one audience considers common knowledge may be considered obscure details by a different audience. For this reason, you need to consider your audience as you draft, and you need to share your drafts with your teacher and peers for feedback about appropriate citations.

WHETHER YOU'RE SHARING THE INTERVIEWS YOU CONDUCTED OR YOUR ANALYSIS OF JOURNAL ARTICLES, YOU'LL NEED TO KNOW HOW TO LET YOUR AUDIENCE KNOW WHAT KIND OF RESEARCH YOU DID AND HOW IT RELATES TO THE LARGER CONVERSATION ABOUT YOUR TOPIC.

You should also consider the cultural context for your writing as you determine how and what to cite. In some cultures, such as the American university culture in which you're currently studying, it's common to cite the original author of a particular sentence, phrase, or even idea, whereas in other cultures, it may be common to draw from the shared knowledge about a topic without citing individual authors. Part of your responsibility as a writer is to learn the common conventions and practices (and your teacher's expectations) for citing your sources in each of your writing situations.

For some projects, your instructor will ask that you cite your sources using a standard citation format such as APA or MLA Style. Some instructors will specify the style that they want you to use while others will leave the choice up to you. Using these standard citation styles will help you to become more familiar with the kinds of information that citations usually include. Even if you'll never have to use MLA or APA in your own academic field, knowing what kinds of information are commonly included in citations will help you better adapt to whatever citation style your future professors or employers may require.

Purdue Libraries Online Interface

The following screenshots will help you navigate the Purdue Libraries website and learn a little more about how to select appropriate search terms in order to find the information you're looking for. Your instructor may refer to this section during in-class activities or may ask you to review this section and complete similar searches using a topic of your choice. Even if your instructor doesn't use this section directly, it will still help you know your options when you begin to conduct secondary research.

The following images and information have been adapted from the Purdue Libraries website <www.lib.purdue.edu> and the CORE tutorial <http://gemini.lib.purdue.edu/core/login/login.cfm>.

SEARCHING THE CATALOG

1. Enter a term in the "Search For" box.

2. Specify the term type in the "Search By" pulldown list.

3. Click "Search Catalog" to start the search.

SEARCH RESULTS

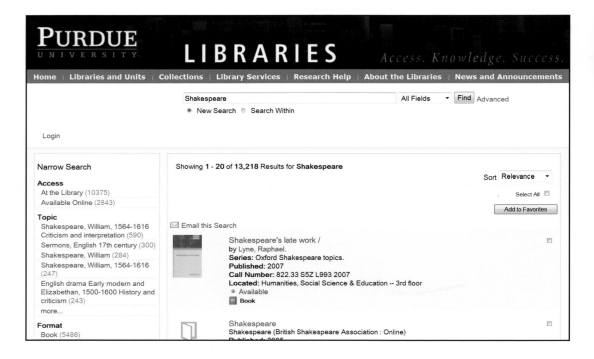

Search Results include the title, author, date, a cover image if available, location, call number, and status. Other information like subject headings are displayed based on the type of search.

SELECTING AN INDIVIDUAL RECORD

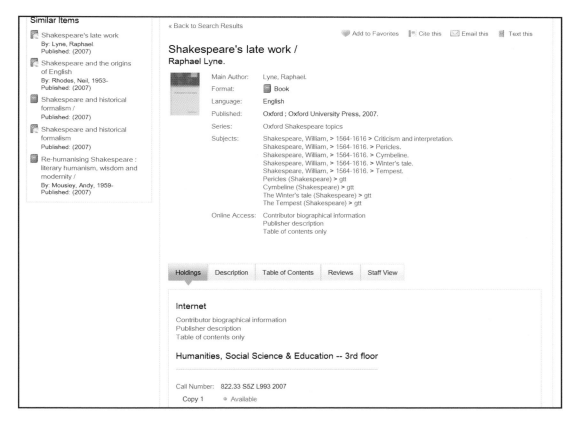

The individual Record includes

- Author's name
- Title of the book
- Place of publication
- Publisher
- Year of publication
- Subjects
- Location
- Call number
- Status

Links throughout the record allow you to conduct a new search within the designated field. In some records, links to an electronic version of the text may also be provided.

FINDING THE PHYSICAL ITEM

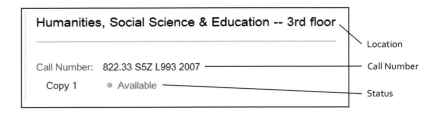

- **Location:** Specifies in which library or unit the resource is located.

- **Call number:** This unique number determines the location of the resource on the book shelves. Most items in the Purdue Libraries have call numbers using the Dewey Decimal Classification or Library of Congress Classification systems.

- **Status:** Provides information on whether the item is checked out or available. If the item you need is checked out, you may request that the item be returned by clicking the "Request This Item" link beside the status field.

SEARCHING FOR ARTICLES

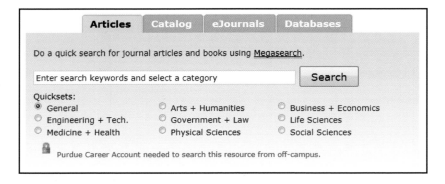

1. Enter a term in the search box.

2. Specify the "Quickset" to select certain databases.

3. Click "Search."

USING "MEGASEARCH"

Megasearch "Simple" Quick Search

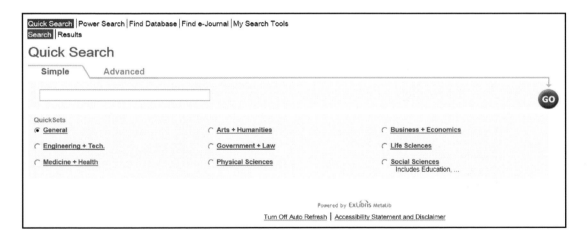

Quick Search is an easy way to search for information in a pre-defined set of databases.

1. Enter a term in the search box.
2. Click "Go" to start the search.

Megasearch "Advanced" Quick Search

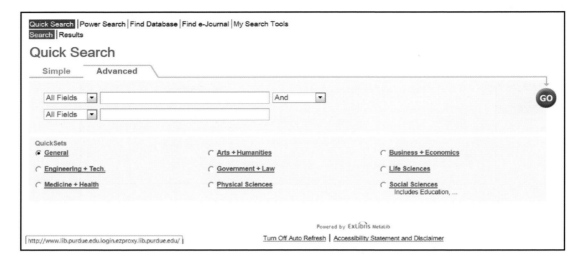

The Advanced Search provides more options for specifying the information for which you are searching. It is possible to compose complex search expressions using field specific searches and Boolean logic.

1. After clicking the "Advanced" tab, two fields are provided for you to specify the information that you seek. Select a field type from the pulldown list on the right of the field.

2. Enter a term in one or both fields.

3. If you filled in both fields, specify the Boolean term to describe the relationship between the two fields.

4. Click "Go" to start the search.

Megasearch "Power Search"

Power Search provides complete control over which databases are searched and provides a variety of options for viewing the results in these databases.

To access, click "Power Search" in the menu. The term Power Search, also known as integrated searching, federated searching, or cross-database searching, means to submit a query to numerous databases at once. The query is broadcast to each database, and an integrated list of the results is displayed from all the databases according to the results' relevancy rank.

1. Select the list of databases you wish to use for your search from the dropdown list in "Select Search Type."

2. Click the checkbox for the specific databases you wish to use for your search.

3. Enter a term in the search box or click the "Advanced" tab, select the relevant search fields, and enter your search term(s).

4. Click "Go" to start the search in the specified databases.

Power Search Results

Power Search Results enable you to view results from the searched databases. You can view the results of a specific database by clicking "results by databases" and then clicking the "View" or "Jump" link of any of the databases in the displayed list. To view the combined results from the searched databases, click "combined results."

Browsing the Results

- Click "Next" or "Previous" to display another page of results. You can set the number of results displayed per page as part of your preferences.

- You can jump to the beginning of the list using the fast back << arrow or jump to the end of the list using the fast forward >> arrow in the Combined Results

- Click the "Title" or the record sequential number to see the record's Full View.

- Click the database name to link to the database's Web site. When possible, the same record is displayed in the database's native interface.

- Click the encircled "+" to save a record in your basket. Your basket is temporary storage for records that you find interesting. You can later move records from the basket to an eShelf folder, save records to disk (in various formats) or email them. Once you add a record to the basket, the icon changes to an encircled "+" with an arrow.

- Click the encircled red "S" to use SFX which provides access to a range of relevant electronic resources, such as the full text of articles or holdings information in your library's OPAC.

"Full View" of a Record

Full View provides all the record's information. It shows a page for each record and highlights the words you queried.

- Click the encircled "+" icon to save a record in your basket. Your basket is a temporary storage for records that you find interesting. At a later stage, you can move records from the basket to an eShelf folder.

- Click the "Find It" button to use SFX which provides access to a range of relevant electronic resources, such as the full text of articles or holdings information in your library's OPAC.

- Click the disk icon, to save the results to a file on your PC.

- Click the envelope icon to email the record.

- Click "Full Text," to link directly to the full text without going through the SFX menu. This option only appears when available.

THE "FIND IT" BUTTON AND THE SFX SERVER

The SFX link server can be accessed through the "Find It" button as well as the encircled red "S" icon.

Clicking on either will bring up a window of the services available through the library for that particular record. For example, links to the full text of an article, to a document delivery service, an ILL form, or a check for print holdings in a catalog. Only the services that are relevant to the record you are looking at appear in the SFX menu.

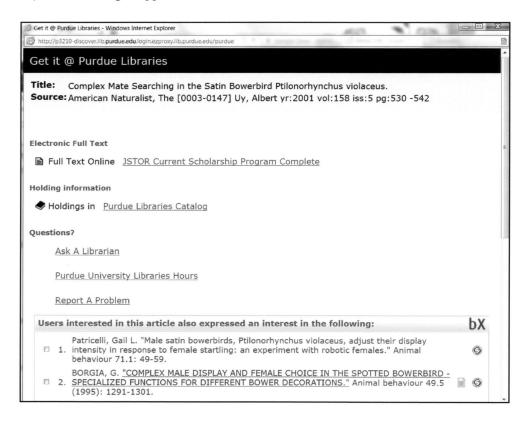

SEARCHING eJOURNALS

1. Search for specific journal titles.

   - Select "Starts with" if entering the first words of the journal's title.
   - Select "Contains" if entering terms contained in the journal's title.

2. Click the "Search" button.

TITLE SEARCH RESULTS

1. Click the journal's title to see all available services for the record.

   OR

2. Click a database title to perform a database search of the title.

SEARCHING DATABASES

To Search a Particular Database

1. Select a database title from the pulldown list.
2. Click "Go."

Databases by Subject

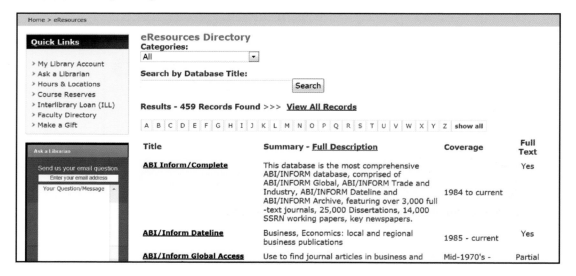

1. Select a database category from the pulldown list.
2. Browse the descriptions for a database best suited to your research.
3. Select the title to search the database.

Multi-subject Databases

If you are not sure which database is the appropriate database for your research topic, start with a multi-subject database. Through these databases, you can find key scholarly journals and controlled vocabulary related to your topic. The following databases are useful:

- **Academic Search Premier**
  Provides access to articles from journals, magazines, and newspapers in a wide range of subject areas. It boasts 3000+ publications, including 1700 peer-reviewed scholarly journals. Over 1200 publications are available in full text.

- **Proquest Research Library**
  Includes access to articles in scholarly journals, trade publications, magazines, and newspaper articles from approximately 4000 publications in a wide variety of subject areas. Full text articles are available from more than 2700 publications.

- **OmniFile Full Text Mega**
  A multi-disciplinary database drawing from literature in more than 3500 publications and full text articles from over 1700 publications.

- **LexisNexis Academic**
  Primarily known for its collection of national and international newspapers and newswires.

- **Newspaper Source**
  Provides cover-to-cover full text for 35 national and international newspapers. Also included are full text news transcripts from major television networks as well as radio shows.

- **JSTOR**
  Full-text digital archive of over 700 scholarly journals.

Database Sample Search: Academic Search Premier

Note: Database hosts vary, thus steps for searching may vary.

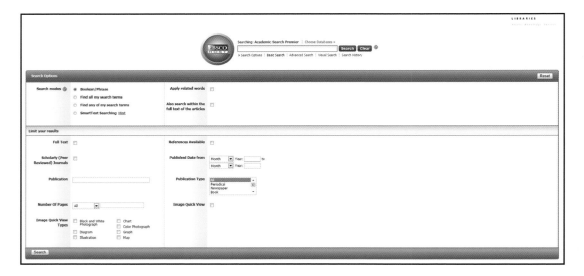

1. Enter terms in the search box.
2. Click "Search." You may select search options or "limit your results" to select only "full text" records or "scholarly (peer reviewed) journals," for instance. You can also search in specific "publications" or according to particular "publication types."

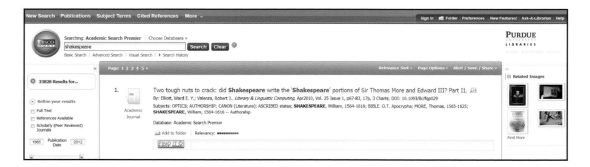

1. Click on a title to retrieve the full record.

   OR

2. Click the "Find It" button to see library services available for the record.

SEARCH STRATEGIES

Creating Search Statements

When searching for information on a particular topic, you must take complex concepts and translate them into search statements appropriate for the search engines you will be using. A search statement makes it possible to search effectively and efficiently for sources related to your topic or thesis statement.

Once you've identified the terms you want to use for searching in a database, the next step is to think about how these terms can be used in conjunction to each other. Combining multiple search terms is a powerful way to retrieve relevant information from a database.

There are two important elements to an effective search statement: relevant search terms and appropriate operators. Operators are words or symbols that are inserted between search terms to instruct the computer on how to search the records.

Search Term Selection

A search term is any word or phrase that is significant or meaningful to your topic. These are the terms you type into the search box of a search engine. Usually, a search term is a noun or an adjective, and sometimes a verb, that are concrete concepts. Avoiding certain terms eliminates irrelevant or unfocused search results.

Use your thesis statement or concept map to highlight the significant words and phrases that convey the major concepts. For instance:

> Instituting **global standards** would ensure immediate and long-term **environmental protection**.

The next step is to create more search terms. Once you have multiple terms you will combine these search terms together in your search statements.

Examples of Related Words		
Global	international	multinational	worldwide
Standards	policy, policies	guidelines	protocols
Environment	ecology	wildlife	ecosystem, ecosystems
Protection	protect, protecting	conservation, conserving	regulation, regulating

Search Terms to Avoid

Some words entered into your search statement may prevent you from retrieving effective search results. The following types of terms are best avoided when selecting your search terms.

Stopwords are words that have a high frequency of use in the English language. Called stopwords because they can slow down or invalidate a search. Many databases and search engines are programmed to ignore these words. Examples:

> articles (a, an, the)
>
> prepositions (of, on, in, with)
>
> conjunctions (but, however)

Common words are often terms so heavily used in a given database that they will retrieve too many records to be useful. For example, using the search term "education" in the *Education Full Text* database would retrieve almost every record in that database.

Abstract words or concepts can be difficult to describe search terms, such as "causes of" or "impact on." These are a reflection, analysis, and evaluation of your research rather than a concrete, descriptive term. Use of these typically generates invalid search results. Some of the abstract terms to avoid include:

impact	development	contrast
influence	significance	cause
importance	comparison	characteristics
effect		

Boolean Operators

Images and text on this page are from: http://gemini.lib.purdue.edu/core/files/strategies1b.html

AND

Now that you've identified multiple search terms, it is time to start combining them together into your search statement. The Boolean Operator AND combines terms together for a more narrow and refined search. This type of search requires *all* terms to appear in each retrieved record and is very similar to an "all of these terms" search in a web search engine.

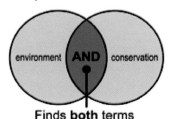

Finds **both** terms

The AND area represents which records would be displayed in the search engine's results list. For best results, use the AND operator to connect major concepts not synonyms.

OR

Another way to combine search terms together is with the Boolean Operator **OR.** The OR operator combines terms together for a broader search. This type of search requires *any* of the search terms to appear in each retrieved record and is very similar to an "any of these terms" search in a web search engine.

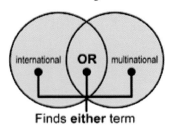

Finds **either** term

This area represents which records would be displayed in the search engine's results list. For best results, use the OR operator to search related terms, synonyms, or variant spellings.

Truncation and Wildcards

Truncation and wildcards broaden your search capabilities by allowing you to retrieve multiple spellings of a root word or word stem, such as singular and plural forms.

A wildcard is a special character, such as an asterisk (*), question mark (?), or pound sign (#), that replaces one or more letters in a word. Truncation is using a wildcard at the end of a root word to search multiple variations of that root word. Check a database's help section to identify what symbol is used for a wildcard.

In this search example: **protect* OR conserv* OR regulat*** would retrieve multiple spellings of these synonyms.

Some databases may allow you to use truncation at the beginning of words or within words (this is called internal truncation). Consult the help files in the database to determine the availability of this feature.

Nesting

Nesting is an advanced search strategy that allows you to combine multiple search terms together and utilize Boolean operators and wildcards. Called nesting because parenthesis are often used to group main concepts together.

Continuing with the example of global environmental protection, a comprehensive search statement would include each of the major concepts of the topic as well as the related terms (synonyms) that you've identified.

A possible nested search statement could be: **(global OR international OR multinational OR worldwide) AND (environment OR ecology) AND (protect* OR conserv* OR regulat*)**

Glossary of Terms

Excerpted from http://www.lib.purdue.edu/rguides/studentinstruction/glossary.html

Article   A contribution written for publication in a journal, magazine, or newspaper. A source of contemporary information.

Call Number   A combination of numbers and letters which identifies a particular book or item in the library's collection. Items are arranged on the book shelves by call number. (See also **Dewey Decimal Classification System**).

Catalog   A database of records representing books, journals, media, government documents, and other materials held in a particular library or location. Online catalogs can usually be searched by various methods, such as author, title, subject, call number, or keyword. Typically, they display the call number and location of the material, with descriptive details.

Database   A collection of information, usually stored in an electronic format that can be searched by a computer.

Dewey Decimal Classification System   A method to classify and shelve items by using numbers and letters to represent subject content. (See also **Call number**).

Field   A part of a record in a database which represents one descriptive or identifying element (such as author, title, subject heading, etc.) for an item. (See also **Database**; **Record**).

Holdings   The materials owned by a library.

Index   (1) A list of names or topics usually found at the end of a publication, which directs the reader to the pages where the names or topics are discussed; (2) A printed or electronic publication which lists references to sources (e.g. periodical articles, books, chapters, etc.) by subject and/or author.

Interlibrary Loan (ILL)   A service that allows you to borrow materials from other libraries through your own library.

Issue   A single numbered or dated publication that is formed when journal, magazine, or newspaper articles are compiled for publication.

Journal   A publication, issued on a regular basis, which contains scholarly research published as articles, papers, research reports, or technical reports. (See also **Magazine**; **Periodicals**).

Keyword   (1) A significant word or term in the title, abstract or text of an item that indicates its subject; (2) A type of search method which retrieves search terms from anywhere in the record. (See also **Free-Text**).

Library of Congress Subject Headings (LCSH)   A list of accepted subject terms developed by the United States Library of Congress, which is used in many library catalogs and some indexes. (See also **Subject Headings**).

Operator   A search modifier used to refine the relationship between your search terms. The three major operators are AND, OR and NOT.

Periodical   Material published regularly such as magazines, journals, and newspapers. (See also **Serial**).

Recall   A request for the return of library material before the due date.

Record   The representation of a particular item in a database. A record is generally divided into various fields, each of which represents a type of information that describes or identifies that item. (See also **Database**; **Field**).

Search Query   Terms or phrases, with operators, that are entered into an online database to search. (See also **Keyword**; **Controlled Vocabulary**).

Serial   A library term for periodicals: items which are published regularly, such as magazines, journals, newspapers, yearbooks, etc. (See also **Periodical**).

Source   A general term that refers to an item or material that provides information.

Stacks   The area where library collections are shelved.

Subject Headings   Accepted terms or phrases used in indexes and library catalogs to group materials on the same topic. (See also **Descriptor**; **Controlled Vocabulary**; **Library of Congress Subject Headings**).

Volume   An item which contains the total collection of all sequential periodical issues over a given time period. (See also **Bound Volume**).

6

Where Can I Publish My ICaP Work?

Purdue Publication Venues

Undergraduate Journals

THE GOAL: BY THE END OF THIS CHAPTER, YOU'LL KNOW WHY YOU SHOULD PUBLISH YOUR WORK AND WHERE YOU CAN PUBLISH YOUR WORK.

Where Can I Publish My ICaP Work?

As you already have or probably will discuss in your ICaP course, publishing your writing (i.e. sharing it with others) can be an important part of the writing process. Making your work visible to others besides yourself, your classroom teacher, and your peer reviewers can be rewarding because it helps you to situate your ideas among others' ideas and to participate in the broader conversation about your topic. When you publish your work, others have the opportunity to respond to it, engage with it, and build on it. When you publish, you don't just learn from others—they learn from you!

Publication is an important part of using writing to further our shared knowledge on any topic. Scholars and researchers often publish their ideas and/or results from experiments by writing articles for academic journals, which allows the knowledge that scholars have gained to be shared with others who don't have direct access to the authors of the article. Your instructor may even ask for your permission to include some of your work in their own scholarship. But publishing isn't just for the professional scholars and researchers. If you've ever used an online discussion forum, you know that by publishing your own results (i.e. how you fixed your own computer when it started making that weird creaking sound), you can distribute knowledge to others who might experience the same problem. If you never publish your writing, you'll miss out on the opportunity to see how writing can help solve public problems or can contribute to public knowledge.

Although becoming a famous researcher who publishes articles in widely-read academic journals might not be on your list of things to do, you can still publish your work, even as a college student, and in the sections that follow, you'll find a few places to consider. If you have a project that you really enjoyed writing or one that you think others might learn from, keep reading and talk to your teacher about the possibility of publishing it in one of the places listed below. It's also possible that your ICaP instructor may design a project that's aimed at one of these publication venues. If so, by the end of the writing process, you'll have a draft of a project that is ready to be considered for publication in one of these venues.

Purdue Publication Venues

PURDUE WRITING SHOWCASE

The Purdue Writing Showcase is a great place to publish your ICaP work in a visual display. The Showcase is a day-long event held each spring that is designed to make the public aware of the outstanding work done by writing students and instructors. Students and instructors create a visual display—a poster, a video, an interactive installation—to explain their writing or research project to the public. This event draws an audience of students and instructors from a variety of writing courses and other members of the Purdue community (faculty, students, and administrators). Although participants do not have to prepare a formal presentation about their project, if you participate, you can expect to talk to visitors about your project on a one to one or small group basis. The Showcase is a great way to share your work with the Purdue community and to understand how a larger audience might respond to your project. It also offers you the chance to win one of the many prizes that are awarded by the ICaP Program.

Frequently Asked Questions about the Purdue Writing Showcase

What is it?
The showcase is a university-wide, day-long event where students and instructors can display their work and view the work of others.

Who can participate?
All ICaP students are eligible for the ICaP Showcase. Students may be nominated by their instructor or may elect to participate independently. Student projects may be individually or collaboratively authored.

What do you mean by "display"?
The showcase is similar to a poster session in that projects will be in poster format, on laptops, or on other interactive media. The idea is to give Showcase guests a visually-oriented overview of the project, allowing them to "get" the project quickly and easily.

What about students who wrote more traditional research papers?
How do they participate? Students might create a poster where they highlight key research questions or findings, or they might represent the research in a visual way, either through collage, selected quotes, or other visual aids.

What needs to go into a display?
Each display should consist of: the project (in poster or other multimedia form); the original assignment; a brief reflection by the student(s); a brief reflection by the instructor. Students also bring their original project to the showcase in case anyone would like to see it, and if students would like to be judged for the award in that category, they will need to turn in the original project ahead of the showcase date to ensure it can be judged.

Who actually creates the display?
Instructors and students typically work together to create the display. The ICaP Program also sponsors workshops to help students work on their displays.

Why should I participate?
At the Showcase, you will be recognized for your work, have the opportunity to discuss your work with others, and be eligible for awards in various project categories.

Frequently Asked Questions about the Purdue Writing Showcase

What are the award categories?

(1) Dean's award
This award will be determined by the Dean or her representative(s) for a work or presentation of particular distinction.

(2) Award for best project in its original form
This award is given to the best project in its original form, regardless of the genre or media used to create the project. To be judged for this award, the original project must be submitted to the ICaP website in advance.

(3) Award for best reflection
This award recognizes the reflection that students write about their course project. To be considered for this award, students should not only include their reflection in their Showcase display but also bring a second copy of their reflection to the Showcase and should submit this additional copy at the registration desk before the Showcase begins.

(4) Award for best display of a project
This award recognizes achievement in the display of the showcased project (i.e. how the presenter has revised the project produced in an ICaP course for display in a public forum in the poster presentation genre).

(5) People's choice award
This award will be determined at the Showcase itself by ballots submitted by attendees.

Currently, the Writing Showcase brings together work in both the Introductory Composition and the Professional Writing Programs at Purdue. Students can present any of the work they completed for an ICaP course.

PURDUE LITERARY AWARDS

The Purdue Literary Awards Contest is sponsored by the Purdue University Department of English, Purdue University Libraries, and the College of Liberal Arts. The contest offers an undergraduate award for the best set of three projects originally written for English 10600 or 10800. The projects may be submitted on CD, in print, or on other physical media. Although this contest is primarily an opportunity to be recognized for a Purdue award, it will allow you to gain a slightly larger audience for your work—other readers associated with the English Department will read the submissions. For more information about the Purdue Literary Awards, you can visit: http://www.cla.purdue.edu/english/literaryawards/index.html

Undergraduate Journals

If you're looking for a somewhere that you can publish your work and receive a wider audience beyond Purdue's campus, you might find that an undergraduate journal is the ideal place to submit your writing project. These journals are often distributed in print and online to a broad audience. For anyone thinking about getting a graduate degree, publishing in an undergraduate journal can also be a great way to see how publication works.

JOURNAL OF PURDUE UNDERGRADUATE RESEARCH

http://docs.lib.purdue.edu/jpur/

"The *Journal of Purdue Undergraduate Research* has been established to publish outstanding research papers written by Purdue undergraduates from all disciplines who have completed faculty-mentored research projects. The journal is run by students, but behind the scenes is a unique partnership between Purdue University Press and other departments of Purdue University Libraries, working with Purdue Marketing and Media and the Online Writing Lab, based in the Department of English. Publication of JPUR is sponsored by the Office of the Provost at Purdue University."

YOUNG SCHOLARS IN WRITING

http://cas.umkc.edu/english/publications/youngscholarsinwriting/default.asp

"*Young Scholars in Writing: Undergraduate Research in Writing and Rhetoric* is a refereed journal dedicated to publishing research articles written by undergraduates in a wide variety of disciplines associated with rhetoric and writing. It is guided by these central beliefs: (1) that research can and should be a crucial component of rhetorical education and (2) that undergraduates engaged in research about writing and rhetoric should have opportunities to share their work with a broader audience of students, scholars, and teachers through national publication. *Young Scholars in Writing* is intended to be a resource for students engaged in undergraduate research and for scholars who are interested in new advances or theories relating to language, composition, rhetoric, and related fields."

UNDERGRADUATE JOURNAL OF SERVICE LEARNING AND COMMUNITY-BASED RESEARCH

http://www.bk.psu.edu/Academics/journal.htm

"The *Undergraduate Journal of Service Learning and Community-Based Research* is a refereed, multi-disciplinary, online undergraduate journal dedicated to publishing intellectual and reflective work by undergraduates on service learning, community-based research, and all related curriculum- and/or research-based community partnerships. Published work will advance knowledge in these subject areas. The editorial team of *Undergraduate Journal of Service Learning and Community-Based Research* encourages undergraduates to pursue their own intellectual projects and to join the academic conversation." This would be especially suited for the kinds of projects that students complete in English 10800: Engaging in Public Discourse.

XCHANGES

http://infohost.nmt.edu/~xchanges/

"*Xchanges* is an interdisciplinary Technical Communication, Writing/Rhetoric, and Writing Across the Curriculum journal, which publishes two issues annually from its home in the Technical Communication program at New Mexico Tech. Our Winter issue each year, published in February, features the theses and research projects of upper-level undergraduate students. We receive submissions (article-length research projects or senior theses) from students from a wide array of institutions across the country. Our faculty review board, comprised of TC, Comp/Rhet, and WAC faculty from throughout the U.S., reviews these submissions on a 'blind' basis. Our second issue of each year, published in November, is an international graduate student issue, the submissions to which are also subject to blind review by our board. We welcome undergraduate and graduate students in these disciplines to submit their work to *Xchanges,* either as traditional articles or as multi-modal 'webtexts.'"

THE SIGMA TAU DELTA REVIEW

http://www.english.org/sigmatd/publications/index.shtml

"*The Sigma Tau Delta Review* (founded in 2005) is an annual journal that publishes critical essays on literature, essays on rhetoric and composition, and essays devoted to pedagogical issues. Manuscripts should not exceed 3,000 words, but exceptions will be made for essays of stellar quality. Critical essays must follow the Modern Language Association style guidelines as defined in the MLA Handbook for Writers of Research Papers (latest edition)."

7

What ICaP and Purdue Policies Should I Know?

Registration: Drop/Add Procedures

Composition Credit Policies

Honors

Permission to Use Student Work

Attendance

Use of Electronic Devices/Cell Phones

Academic Honesty

ICaP Student Decorum Policy

Conflicts and Complaints

Grades

Purdue University Nondiscrimination Policy

Disability Resource Center Accommodations

Copyright Materials

Campus Emergencies

THE GOAL: BY THE END OF THIS CHAPTER, YOU'LL KNOW THE IMPORTANT ICaP AND PURDUE POLICIES RELATED TO TOPICS SUCH AS ATTENDANCE, GRADING, EMERGENCY PROCEDURES, AND STUDENT DECORUM.

What ICaP and University Policies Should I Know?

The following policies come from either University Regulations or from the ICaP Program Policy Statements. In addition to the policies written here, your instructor will have policies that are specific to your composition class. Please read your course syllabus and refer to it regularly for your class objectives, requirements and expectations.

Registration: Drop/Add Procedures

During the first week of the semester, you may add or drop any class that has space available using the mypurdue online registration. Composition courses have strict course limits, so ICaP instructors will not sign you into their classes during the first week.

ICaP instructors will not sign you into their classes after the first week of the semester either; it is against ICaP policy for them to do so, so please don't ask. Composition courses begin readings and writing assignments the first week, and the pace of the course is fast. Of course you believe you can "catch up," but that rarely works. Your instructor has a lot of material to cover in 16 short weeks. The foundation instructors set the first week is important, so you shouldn't miss it.

Course Additions	
Week 1	You may do web registrations with no approval needed; you are strongly encouraged to consult with your academic advisor before adding a class.
Weeks 2–4	You may not add an ICaP class after the first week. If you have been cancelled from your classes by the university (from non-payment of fees), take a copy of your original schedule and a Form 23 to the assistant director of ICaP for approval to add. (For non-ICaP classes, you must have approval from your academic advisor and instructor before adding a class.)
Weeks 5–9	Adding an ICaP class at this time is unlikely for any reason. The only way you can add any class is if you have extenuating circumstances and only with approval of an academic advisor, the instructor, and the head of the department in which the course is listed.
Weeks 10–16	Course additions are not permitted.

Course Drops	
Weeks 1–2	You may drop courses with no approval from anyone. You are strongly encouraged to consult with your academic advisor before dropping a class.
Weeks 3–4	You may drop with approval from your academic advisor. The drop will be recorded with a grade of W (withdraw).
Weeks 5–9	You may drop with the approval from your academic advisor. Instructors must indicate with their signature (on a Form 23) whether you are passing or failing, and a grade of W, WF, WN, or WU will be recorded. If you have a semester classification of 0 and fewer than 31 hours of college credit, OR you have a semester classification of 01 or 02, you need not have the instructor's signature. Your grade will be recorded as W.
Weeks 10–16	Course assignments cannot be cancelled during this period.

Composition Credit Policies

There is no test-out for First-Year Composition.

If you took the English *Language* and Composition Advanced Placement (AP) Exam and received a score of 4 or 5, you *may* already have credit for English 10600. Please see your academic advisor right away. If you took the English *Literature* and Composition AP Exam, you *do NOT* get credit for English 10600.

THERE IS NO TEST-OUT FOR FIRST-YEAR COMPOSITION.

Honors

Composition courses may not be taken for honors credit. Honors courses are taught only by faculty members, and composition courses are largely taught by graduate instructors who are not members of the faculty.

Permission to Use Student Work

In the first two weeks of the semester, your instructor will ask you to tear out and hand in the "Permission to Use Student Work" form from page 101 of this book. If you sign this form, you allow your instructor to use your writing as an example in teaching and research. You are under no obligation to allow your instructor to use your work, and your decision will have no influence on your grade in the class. The form gives you options and conditions under which you would allow your work to be used.

Attendance

You are expected to be present every day your class is scheduled, and you can expect your instructor to be present for every class meeting that is listed on your course schedule. If your instructor must cancel class, he or she will contact you through email or will post a message on the course website. If your class is held in Heavilon Hall, your instructor will ask the ICaP secretary to put a sign on the door stating that your class has been cancelled for the day.

Your instructor should be in the classroom when class begins. If your instructor does not show up 10 minutes after class is scheduled to start, one student should call the ICaP office (494-3730) or the English Department Office (494-3740) and ask if the instructor has cancelled class.

ATTENDANCE IN CONFERENCES

YOU SHOULD ALWAYS MEET FOR YOUR SCHEDULED CONFERENCE IN EITHER HEAVILON HALL ROOM 223 OR 225, NOT IN THE UNION OR IN YOUR INSTRUCTOR'S OFFICE.

If you are in English 10600, your class schedule indicates that you will meet in either HEAV 223 or 225 for conferences every week. In reality, you may meet every week or every other week for conferences, and you may have group meetings or individual conferences. Your instructor will give you a detailed conference schedule, but you should be in conferences at least once every other week, so reserve this time on your personal schedule. You should always meet for your scheduled conference in either Heavilon Hall Room 223 or 225, not in the Union or in your instructor's office.

ATTENDANCE IN THE CLASSROOM

Unless your instructor has scheduled a supplementary computer lab time or a library trip, you should meet in the classroom or lab that's listed on your schedule. If you are meeting somewhere else, you should be notified through email and the new venue will be listed on your course website.

PURDUE UNIVERSITY'S ATTENDANCE POLICY

Students are expected to be present for every meeting of the classes in which they are enrolled. Only the instructor can excuse a student from a course requirement or responsibility. When conflicts or absences can be anticipated, such as for many University sponsored activities and religious observations, the student should inform the instructor of the situation as far in advance as possible. For unanticipated or emergency absences when advance notification to an instructor is not possible, the student should contact the instructor as soon as possible by email, or by contacting the main office that offers the course. When the student is unable to make direct contact with the instructor and is unable to leave word with the instructor's department because of circumstances beyond the student's control, and in cases of bereavement, the student or the student's representative should contact the Office of the Dean of Students. (See Grief Absence Policy Statement in the next section.)

> **FOR UNANTICIPATED OR EMERGENCY ABSENCES, THE STUDENT SHOULD CONTACT THE INTRUCTOR AS SOON AS POSSIBLE BY EMAIL, OR BY CONTACTING THE MAIN OFFICE THAT OFFERS THE COURSE.**

The link to the complete policy and implications can be found at http://www.purdue.edu/odos/services/classabsence.htm

PURDUE UNIVERSITY'S GRIEF ABSENCE POLICY: EFFECTIVE JULY 1, 2011

Purdue University recognizes that a time of bereavement is very difficult for a student. The University therefore provides the following rights to students facing the loss of a family member through the Grief Absence Policy for Students (GAPS). GAPS Policy: Students will be excused for funeral leave and given the opportunity to earn equivalent credit and to demonstrate evidence of meeting the learning outcomes for missed assignments or assessments in the event of the death of a member of the student's family.

A student should contact the ODOS to request that a notice of his or her leave be sent to instructors. The student will provide documentation of the death or funeral service attended to the ODOS. Given proper documentation, the instructor will excuse the student from class and provide the opportunity to earn equivalent credit and to demonstrate evidence of meeting the learning outcomes for missed assignments or assessments. If the student is not satisfied with the implementation of this policy by a faculty member, he or she is encouraged to contact the Department Head and if necessary, the ODOS, for further review of his or her case. In a case where grades are negatively affected, the student may follow the established grade appeals process.

Purdue University's entire Grief Absence Policy is available at http://www.purdue.edu/odos/services/griefabsencepolicyforstudents.php

Use of Electronic Devices/Cell Phones

YOU SHOULD NOT BE TEXTING, PLAYING COMPUTER GAMES, DOING HOMEWORK FOR OTHER COURSES, OR CHECKING EMAIL OR SOCIAL MEDIA SITES UNLESS YOU ARE DOING SO AS PART OF A CLASS ACTIVITY.

Laptops and smartphones are welcome in the classroom, but only as appropriately used educational tools. Your instructor needs to maintain a classroom environment without disruptions, so while you are in your composition class, keep your attention on the activities and tasks going on in the classroom. You should not be texting, playing computer games, doing homework for other courses, or checking email or social media sites unless you are doing so as part of a class activity. The ringer on your cell phone should be silent, and other students should not be able to hear your phone vibrate on the desk or table. Your instructor may ask you to keep your cell phone in your backpack or pocket to avoid distractions.

Appropriate use of laptops and smartphones in the classroom may include:

- Reading online texts or textbooks.
- Researching articles or websites.
- Taking notes.
- Writing drafts.
- Completing peer reviews.
- Receiving emergency text messages.

The university communicates emergency information to students, faculty, and staff who have signed up with the Emergency Warning Notification System: *Purdue ALERT.* In cases of threatening weather or other dangers to the campus community, the university will send text messages. Therefore, at least one person in every room should have the ability to receive emergency text messages. *(Whether or not you are going to this weekend's football game is not an emergent situation.)*

Academic Honesty

Your instructor will have a complete definition of plagiarism on your course syllabus, and you can expect to have discussions in class on how to properly cite sources which you have summarized, paraphrased or quoted. During the first nine weeks of the semester, your instructor will explain what plagiarism is and how to avoid plagiarizing others' work. As you are learning how to take careful notes and to attribute your sources, you may make errors based on misunderstanding what plagiarism is or how to cite sources. Your instructor will address your errors of misunderstanding or carelessness as correctable and teachable moments. You may need to revise your assignment (perhaps for a reduced score), and you may meet with your instructor in conference or office hours to further discuss plagiarism and its consequences.

If, after you have discussed academic honesty in class, you copy and paste sections from other sources without attribution (also known as "patch writing"), if you paraphrase without attribution, or if you fail to heed the in-class lessons on attribution, your instructor may fail your paper or project and file a report with the Dean of Students.

There is no doubt that handing in someone else's written work as your own is dishonest and wrong. Therefore, if you commit *egregious* acts of plagiarism, even in the first nine weeks of the semester, your instructor may file a report with the Office of the Dean of Students. Additionally, you may fail your paper and depending on the policies your instructor has on the class syllabus, you may fail the course. If you commit an egregious act of plagiarism beyond the ninth week of the semester, you have clearly violated Purdue's Academic Integrity Policy. At this point, your instructor may see that you have missed your "teachable moment" in the current semester and you will receive a grade of F (failing) for the course.

Egregious acts of plagiarism include:

- Purchasing or "borrowing" essays.

- Purchasing essays from a Paper Mill.

- Using parts of a Paper Mill essay (such as copying and pasting the parts you can see without paying for the entire paper).

- Lifting major parts of your paper from sources (without documentation).

- Translating a foreign language article.

- "Patch writing" large amounts of your paper.

- Faking citations, sources, or quotes.

- Taking, stealing, or "borrowing" a paper from a friend, organization, or from a local database of essays.

- Any act of obvious academic dishonesty.

The English Department's definition of plagiarism is:

> When writers use material from other sources, they must acknowledge this source. Not doing so is called plagiarism, which means using without credit the ideas or expression of another. You are therefore cautioned (1) against using, word for word, without acknowledgement, phrases, sentences, paragraphs, etc. from the printed or manuscript material of others; (2) against using with only slight changes the materials of another; (3) against using the general plan, the main headings, or a rewritten form of someone else's material. These cautions apply to the work of other students as well as to the published work of professional writers.

Penalties for plagiarism vary from failure of the plagiarized assignment to expulsion from the university, and may include failure for the course and notification of the Dean of Students' Office. The Department of English considers the previous explanation to be official notification of the nature and seriousness of plagiarism.

PURDUE UNIVERSITY'S REGULATION ON ACADEMIC DISHONESTY

Purdue prohibits "dishonesty in connection with any University activity. Cheating, plagiarism, or knowingly furnishing false information to the University are examples of dishonesty" (Student Conduct Section-B-2-a, University Regulations). Such behavior is subject to disciplinary sanctions. Furthermore, the University Senate has stipulated that "the commitment of acts of cheating, lying, and deceit in any of their diverse forms (such as the use of substitutes for taking examinations, the use of illegal cribs, plagiarism, and copying during examinations) is dishonest and must not be tolerated. Moreover, knowingly to aid and abet, directly or indirectly, other parties in committing dishonest acts is in itself dishonest" (University Senate Document 72-18, December 15, 1972).

The following websites further explain Purdue's regulations on student conduct.

> Purdue University's Student Conduct Code at
> http://www.purdue.edu/univregs/studentconduct/regulations.html

> The Dean of Students' "Academic Integrity: A Guide for Students" at
> http://www.purdue.edu/odos/osrr/academicintegritybrochure.php

ICaP Student Decorum Policy

YOUR RIGHTS AS A STUDENT IN YOUR COMPOSITION COURSE

All students at Purdue are expected to abide by the university's Code of Conduct. The Introductory Composition at Purdue (ICaP) Student Decorum Policy further explains how Purdue's Code of Conduct applies to the specific classroom situations and environments that students in all ICaP courses share.

Who should read this policy?

- Students, to understand the etiquette of college classroom behavior and to be aware of the consequences of inappropriate actions.

- Instructors, to enforce program-specific and university policies consistently.

- Administrators, to support instructors and students when behavioral issues arise.

What is Decorum in the ICaP Classroom?

While we do want our classrooms to be spaces of open discussion and dialogue, students must be aware that their speech and compositions act as part of the larger classroom discourse, and thus have effects and repercussions beyond their own personal experience in the class, and even beyond the teacher-student relationship within the class.

We want to foster an environment where everyone (regardless of nationality, sex, sexual orientation, etc.) is free to express their views without fear of intimidation, unless that expression impinges on others' ability to do so. This requires that we provide others in the classroom with the ability to express their views in a safe environment, and recognize one's own responsibility to contribute to the safety of that environment. The environment of the classroom includes not solely larger class discussion, but also working with groups, course projects, course activities, and conduct in online spaces (forums, online discussions, blogs).

What is Inappropriate Behavior in the English ICaP Classroom?

The following are examples of inappropriate behavior which will not be tolerated in any ICaP classroom:

- Causing or threatening to cause bodily harm to other students or to the instructor.
- Hate speech, including producing written work or images that promote or support hate crimes.
- Gratuitously sexual or violent texts.
- Sexually harassing other students or the instructor.
- Attempts to intimidate other students or the instructor, i.e. harassment, bullying.
- Classroom disruptions, or behaviors that interfere with the educational environment for other students.

What are Classroom Disruptions?

According to the Office of Student Rights and Responsibilities, disruptive behavior is "repeated, continuous, or multiple student behaviors that prevent an instructor from teaching and/or prevent students from learning." (http://www.purdue.edu/odos/osrr/classroombehaviorbrochure.php)

Disruptive classroom behavior can target either students or the instructor and can include conduct during class projects, in-class activities, and within online environments. In these cases, while harassment can be a single, egregious instance, disruption might better be defined by its accumulation—that is, continuous and deliberately done. Examples include:

- Language or behavior that offends or would prevent other students from feeling safe to express themselves in the classroom.

- Continual and heedless "hijacking" of discussions through interruption and distraction.

- Inappropriate use of computers, laptops, cell phones, mp3 players, or other technological devices.

INSTRUCTORS EXPECT STUDENTS TO EXPRESS OPINIONS RESPECTFULLY AND WITHOUT DISRUPTING THE LEARNING PROCESSES OF OTHERS.

What happens when students act inappropriately in the classroom?

ICaP instructors expect their students to be curious learners, to ask questions, and to offer their ideas and thoughts, often in open classroom discussions. And while instructors expect students to have different opinions, they expect students to express those opinions respectfully and without disrupting the learning processes of others. In accordance with that goal, instructors will resolve classroom behavior problems according to the following chart:

	Student Behavior: Mildly inappropriate, disruptive, unprofessional. Disrupts the learning of others.	**Student Behavior:** Egregiously inappropriate or disruptive, potentially harmful to self and/or others.
Step 1	The instructor may address the disruptive behavior. The instructor will issue a verbal warning to the student.	The student may be asked to leave the classroom and the instructor will immediately talk with an administrator in the ICaP office. The instructor will file a Student Conduct Form. Depending on the infraction, the student may be reported to the Office of the Dean of Students. If the instructor feels threatened and is concerned for his or her own safety, the safety of the students, or the safety of the disruptive student, the instructor should call the Purdue Police.

Step 2	Repeated inappropriate behavior: the instructor may ask the student to leave the classroom and take an absence for the day. The instructor will remind the student that this is a repeated offense. The instructor will document the incident and may contact an administrator in the ICaP office to file a Student Conduct Form.	If egregiously inappropriate, disruptive, or potentially harmful behavior continues, the instructor and Program Director will ask the Office of the Dean of Students to investigate the matter.
Step 3	The instructor will inform the student that this is a repeated documented offense. The instructor will contact an administrator in the ICaP office and file a Student Conduct Form.	
Step 4	Depending on the infraction the instructor or the Program Director may call and/or send a written report to the Office of the Dean of Students.	

The entire text of Purdue University's Student Code of Conduct is available at http://www.purdue.edu/univregs/studentconduct/regulations.html

RELATED DEFINITIONS

These definitions are excerpted from Purdue University's Policies on Ethics which include Harassment, Racial Harassment, and Sexual Harassment and are located at http://www.purdue.edu/policies/ethics/iiic1.html

Purdue defines **Harassment** as

> Conduct towards another person or identifiable group of persons that has the purpose or effect of:
>
> - Creating an intimidating or hostile educational environment, or
> - Unreasonably interfering with or affecting a person's educational environment or opportunities.
>
> Use of the term Harassment includes all forms of harassment, including Racial Harassment and Sexual Harassment.

Purdue defines **Racial Harassment** as

> Conduct that demonstrates hostility towards another person (or identifiable group of persons) on the basis of race, color, national origin or ancestry and that has the purpose or effect of:
>
> - Creating an intimidating or hostile educational environment, or
> - Unreasonably interfering with or affecting a person's educational environment or opportunities.

Purdue defines **Sexual Harassment** as

> 1. Any act of Sexual Violence.
> 2. Any act of Sexual Exploitation.
> 3. Any unwelcome sexual advance, request for sexual favors or other written, verbal or physical conduct of a sexual nature when:
>   a. Submission to such conduct is made either explicitly or implicitly a term or condition of an individual's education.
>   b. Submission to, or rejection of, such conduct by an individual is used as the basis for, or a factor in, decisions affecting that individual's education, or
>   c. Such conduct has the purpose or effect of unreasonably interfering with an individual's academic performance or creating an intimidating, offensive or hostile environment for that individual's education.

Purdue University's Violent Behavior Policy is located at http://www.purdue.edu/policies/facilities-safety/iva3.html

Purdue defines **violent behavior** as

> a broad range of behaviors that generate reasonable concerns for personal safety, result in physical injury or result in damage to University Facilities. Violent behavior includes, but is not limited to, aggressive or frightening acts, Intimidation, Threats, Physical Attacks or Property Damage. Threat is defined as "An expression of intent to cause physical or mental harm or damage to property. A threat may be direct, indirect, conditional or veiled. Any threat is presumed to constitute a statement of intent. An expression constitutes a threat without regard to whether the party communicating the threat has the present ability to carry it out and without regard to whether the expression is contingent or future."

Purdue University students who violate this policy on or off University Facilities may be subject to disciplinary action up to and including expulsion, as provided in the Regulations Governing Student Conduct.

Conflicts and Complaints

If you are having a problem in your composition class, you should first try to talk with your instructor. But if you are having a conflict with your instructor, you have a complaint about your class or your instructor, or if you have any question or concern about your composition class, please contact Linda Haynes, the Assistant Director of Composition for Student Concerns (lhaynes@purdue.edu).

Grades

You will receive feedback from your instructor in the form of written and/or verbal comments on your work that will help you revise and improve your writing and composing, but at some point, your instructor will assign a grade to your paper or project. Assigning grades is how instructors give you an evaluation of your work, and you will receive these grades throughout the semester. Even if you are handing in a portfolio at the end of the semester, you should have an idea of where you stand grade-wise at any time during the semester. If your instructor does not use Blackboard or display your grades on a course management system, you can keep track of the graded work that's been returned to you using the "Tracking Your Progress" chart on page xvi.

Most instructors grade your papers with either the number of points you earned for the assignment (and out of how many points) or with a percentage grade. Your instructor will include on your syllabus how much each assignment or project is worth. With each project or major writing assignment, your instructor will give you an explanation of how your compositions are being assessed.

Your instructor will include on the course syllabus whether your final course grade will be a regular A, B, C, D, F letter grade or whether you will be on the +/- grading system. If your instructor uses the +/- system, then all of your graded pieces will also be graded as such.

WHAT GRADES MEAN

The following section offers you some meaning behind the letter grades and points your instructor will use while assessing your work.

The A range

You did what the assignment asked at a high quality level, and your work shows originality and creativity. Work in this range shows all the qualities listed above for a B; but it also demonstrates that you took extra steps to be original or creative in developing content, solving a problem, or developing a verbal or visual style.

The B range

You did what the assignment asked of you at a high quality level. Work in this range needs little revision, is complete in content, is organized well, and shows special attention to style and visual design.

The C range

You did what the assignment asked of you. Work in this range tends to need some revision, but it is complete in content and the organization is logical. The style, verbal and visual, is straightforward but unremarkable.

The D range

You did what the assignment asked at a low level of quality. Work in this range tends to need significant revision. The content is often incomplete and the organization is hard to discern. Verbal and visual style is often non-existent or chaotic.

F

A grade of F is generally for students who don't show up or don't do the work. If you feel you put in your best effort and still received an F, you might consider dropping the class.

Grades of Incomplete

A grade of incomplete is given to a student only under extenuating circumstances beyond a student's control, such as a serious illness or accident. Purdue's University Regulations states, "A grade of incomplete is a record of work that was interrupted by unavoidable absence or other causes beyond a student's control, which work was passing at the time it was interrupted and the completion of which does not require the student to repeat the course in order to obtain credit. The incomplete grade is not to be used as a substitute for a failing grade." If you are in a situation in which you do need an incomplete, you should first talk to someone in the Office of the Dean of Students to have your extended absence recorded.

KEEPING TRACK OF AND GETTING YOUR GRADES

At the end of the semester, you will see your final grade on mypurdue, but you should have some idea of where you stand in the course throughout the semester. Your instructor may use the gradebook in Blackboard or in the Drupal course management system, but instructors are not required to use these features. You should keep track of your own scores as you receive returned graded work from your instructor. As you accumulate your graded papers, quizzes, and assignments, write down the scores using the gradebook in the front of this book. (See "Tracking Your Progress: Composing Your Own Gradebook," on page xvi.)

According to the Family Educational Rights and Privacy Act (FERPA), your instructor may **not** post your grades in a public area that lists your name or even a portion of your PUID. Your instructor is also not allowed to email grades to you.

GRADE APPEALS

University Regulations states that

> The grade appeals system affords recourse to a student who has evidence or believes that evidence exists to show that an inappropriate grade has been assigned as a result of prejudice, caprices, or other improper conditions such as mechanical error, or assignment of a grade inconsistent with those assigned to other students. Additionally, a student may challenge the reduction of a grade for alleged scholastic dishonesty. In essence, the grade appeals system is designed to protect students from grade assignments that are inconsistent with policy followed in assigning grades to others in the course.

PROCEDURE FOR ICAP GRADE REVIEWS

If you wish to challenge a final course grade, you must first discuss the situation with your instructor. If you are not satisfied with the results of that meeting, you may then request an ICaP Grade Review. If you are not satisfied with the decision made by the ICaP Grade Review, you may then speak with the Head of the Department of English and then appeal your grade through the College of Liberal Arts (CLA).

Step One: Contact your instructor.

It is your right to know how your grades are figured, so your first step is to visit, call, or email your instructor to discuss your grade. In some cases, a scoring error may have happened, which can be easily fixed. Or, your instructor can explain how he/she arrived at the grade you received.

Step Two: Submit a completed ICaP Grade Review form, the package of your graded materials, and a cover letter to the Writing Programs Secretary in Heavilon 302.

ICaP Grade Review forms are available in the ICaP office (HEAV 302) and are downloadable on the ICaP website (http://digitalparlor.org/icap/student). The grade review package you submit should include all of your graded work for the class, including teacher comments. We will not accept items that do not show comments from the teacher. Also, write a 1–2 page cover letter that explains why you believe the grade you received does not reflect your work in the class. See the checklist on the grade review form for more information.

Step Three: Wait a week.

We will respond to your grade review in written form within one week. Then, you can pick up the response and your materials at the desk of the Writing Programs Secretary in Heavilon 302.

If we determine a higher grade is warranted, we will make the change automatically through the Office of the Registrar. You should see the new grade reflected soon afterward in your records. **Under no circumstances will your grade be lowered as a result of your work being reviewed or regraded.**

ICaP Grade Review requests must be submitted before or during the third week after the start of the following regular semester. We will not accept requests that arrive after 3:00PM on Friday of the third week of the following semester in which you received your grade.

If you have concerns about your composition class at any time during the semester, please see Linda Haynes, Assistant Director of Composition in Heavilon 303E (lhaynes@purdue.edu).

If you are not satisfied with the results of your grade review, you may take your appeal to the Head of the Department of English.

Purdue University Nondiscrimination Policy

Purdue University is committed to maintaining a community which recognizes and values the inherent worth and dignity of every person; fosters tolerance, sensitivity, understanding, and mutual respect among its members; and encourages each individual to strive to reach his or her own potential. In pursuit of its goal of academic excellence, the University seeks to develop and nurture diversity. The University believes that diversity among its many members strengthens the institution, stimulates creativity, promotes the exchange of ideas, and enriches campus life.

PURDUE UNIVERSITY PROHIBITS DISCRIMINATION AGAINST ANY MEMBER OF THE UNIVERSITY COMMUNITY ON THE BASIS OF RACE, RELIGION, COLOR, SEX, AGE, NATIONAL ORIGIN OR ANCESTRY, MARITAL STATUS, PARENTAL STATUS, SEXUAL ORIENTATION, DISABILITY, OR STATUS AS A VETERAN.

Purdue University prohibits discrimination against any member of the University community on the basis of race, religion, color, sex, age, national origin or ancestry, marital status, parental status, sexual orientation, disability, or status as a veteran. The University will conduct its programs, services and activities consistent with applicable federal, state and local laws, regulations and orders and in conformance with the procedures and limitations as set forth in Executive Memorandum No. D-1, which provides specific contractual rights and remedies.

Disability Resource Center Accommodations

Purdue University is required to respond to the needs of students with disabilities as outlined in both the Rehabilitation Act of 1973 and the Americans with Disabilities Act of 1990 through the provision of auxiliary aids and services that allow a student with a disability to fully access and participate in the programs, services, and activities at Purdue University.

If you have a disability that requires special academic accommodation, please make an appointment to speak with your instructor within the first three (3) weeks of the semester in order to discuss any adjustments. It is important that you talk about this at the beginning of the semester. It is your responsibility to notify the Disability Resource Center (http://www.purdue.edu/drc) of an impairment or condition that may require accommodations and/or classroom modifications.

Copyright Materials

The notes you take in class are considered to be "derivative works" of your instructor's lectures or class materials and therefore may be subject to copyright laws. You are allowed to take notes in class and to use those notes for any non-commercial use, but you are not allowed to sell or barter your class notes without permission from your instructor.

Take notes, please! And feel free to use your class notes to study either individually or in groups, but remember—you are not permitted to receive payment or material goods in return for your notes.

Campus Emergencies

In the event of a major campus emergency, course requirements, deadlines and grading percentages are subject to changes that may be necessitated by a revised semester calendar or other circumstances beyond the instructor's control. Relevant changes to your course will be posted onto the course website or can be obtained by contacting your instructor via email or phone. **You are expected to read your @purdue.edu email on a frequent basis.**

EMERGENCY NOTIFICATION

The *Purdue ALERT* system uses several methods to communicate imminent danger to students. In case of threatening weather, civil disturbance, or release of hazardous materials, you may hear the "All Hazards Emergency Warning Sirens" (the outdoor sirens) which mean you should seek shelter in a safe location within a building. In Heavilon Hall, the Emergency Warning Sirens are not audible. Therefore, it is a good idea to sign up with *Purdue ALERT* so you can receive emergency notifications through text messages.

If you hear a Fire Alarm, you should immediately evacuate the building using the nearest exit and move away from the building until emergency response personnel tell you it is safe to return.

According to Purdue ALERT, "When you hear either emergency warning notification system you should immediately evacuate or go inside a building to a safe location (as applicable) and use all communication means available to find out more details about the emergency. You should remain in place until police, fire, or other emergency response personnel provide additional guidance or tell you it is safe to leave."

Number of Purdue Police: 765-494-8221 for non-emergencies

Email for Purdue Police: police@purdue.edu (not monitored 24 hours/day)

For any emergency, call 911.

Appendix

 **Permission Form**

Dear Student:

Because it is helpful to be able to use student writing as examples in teaching and research, I am asking you for permission to reproduce the writing you do this semester. If you grant me this permission, I might use your writing in several ways:

- I might include it in a showcase of student work on our class website or nominate it for inclusion in the Introductory Composition at Purdue (ICaP) showcase.

- I might photocopy or make a transparency of a paper you write to serve as an example in class, either this semester or sometime in the future.

- I might quote a passage of your writing in a conference paper or an article in a professional journal.

- I might use your paper as an example in a textbook sometime in the future.

Of course, it is also quite possible that I will not use your work, even if you give me permission to do so.

You are under no obligation to allow me to use your work, and your decision will, of course, have no influence on your grade in this class. If you are willing to allow me to reproduce your writing, please fill out the appropriate items on the bottom of this sheet and return it to me. If you decide to grant me permission to use your work, you may withdraw that permission for any specific writing you submit.

Thank you for your consideration and help.

_____

ICaP Instructor

see reverse

TO: _____

You have my permission to use my writing from this course as examples in writing courses, teaching workshops, professional publications, and/or textbooks.

Please check one of the following:

_____ You may use my first and last name to identify my work.

_____ You may use my first name only.

_____ You may use my work, but not my name.
(If you check this option, I will either use your work without any name or I will make up a name.)

In addition, please check below if you wish identifiable features to be changed:

_____ You may use my work, but please change any identifiable details, such as last names of people.

Signature: _____

Printed name: _____

Date: _____

Course, Section, and CRN: _____

 introductory
composition
at purdue

English 106 Pre-Conference Preparation Notes

Date _____/_____/_____

Name _____ Group: A ☐ B ☐

My goal for this conference is to:

Questions/comments I have about my conference assignment:

I have completed this much of the current project so far. (Circle amount completed below.)

Done 100%   90   80   70   60   50   40   30   20   10%   Not started

I have the following technical or computer-related problems or questions:

I have the following grammatical or writing process problems or questions:

News from my life you need to know which could affect my classroom performance:

One thing I could use some help understanding is:

Pre-Conference Form
(to be filled out before your conference)

introductory
composition
at purdue

02

English 106 Pre-Conference Preparation Notes

Date _____ / _____ / _____

Name _____   Group: A ☐   B ☐

My goal for this conference is to:

Questions/comments I have about my conference assignment:

I have completed this much of the current project so far. (Circle amount completed below.)

Done 100%   90   80   70   60   50   40   30   20   10%   Not started

I have the following technical or computer-related problems or questions:

I have the following grammatical or writing process problems or questions:

News from my life you need to know which could affect my classroom performance:

One thing I could use some help understanding is:

03

_____

English 106 Pre-Conference Preparation Notes

Date _____ / _____ / _____

Name _____   Group: A ☐   B ☐

My goal for this conference is to:

Questions/comments I have about my conference assignment:

I have completed this much of the current project so far. (Circle amount completed below.)

   Done 100%   90   80   70   60   50   40   30   20   10%   Not started

I have the following technical or computer-related problems or questions:

I have the following grammatical or writing process problems or questions:

News from my life you need to know which could affect my classroom performance:

One thing I could use some help understanding is:

_____

Pre-Conference Form
(to be filled out before your conference)

04

English 106 Pre-Conference Preparation Notes

Date _____/_____/_____

Name _____   Group: A ☐   B ☐

My goal for this conference is to:

Questions/comments I have about my conference assignment:

I have completed this much of the current project so far. (Circle amount completed below.)

   Done 100%   90   80   70   60   50   40   30   20   10%   Not started

I have the following technical or computer-related problems or questions:

I have the following grammatical or writing process problems or questions:

News from my life you need to know which could affect my classroom performance:

One thing I could use some help understanding is:

Pre-Conference Form
(to be filled out before your conference)

icap introductory composition at purdue

05

_____

English 106 Pre-Conference Preparation Notes

Date _____/_____/_____

Name _____   Group: A ☐   B ☐

My goal for this conference is to:

Questions/comments I have about my conference assignment:

I have completed this much of the current project so far. (Circle amount completed below.)

Done 100%   90   80   70   60   50   40   30   20   10%   Not started

I have the following technical or computer-related problems or questions:

I have the following grammatical or writing process problems or questions:

News from my life you need to know which could affect my classroom performance:

One thing I could use some help understanding is:

_____

Pre-Conference Form
(to be filled out before your conference)

introductory
composition
at purdue

06

English 106 Pre-Conference Preparation Notes

Date _____ / _____ / _____

Name _____ Group: A ☐   B ☐

My goal for this conference is to:

Questions/comments I have about my conference assignment:

I have completed this much of the current project so far. (Circle amount completed below.)

Done 100%   90   80   70   60   50   40   30   20   10%   Not started

I have the following technical or computer-related problems or questions:

I have the following grammatical or writing process problems or questions:

News from my life you need to know which could affect my classroom performance:

One thing I could use some help understanding is:

Pre-Conference Form
(to be filled out before your conference)

07

English 106 Pre-Conference Preparation Notes

Date _____/_____/_____

Name _____   Group: A ☐ B ☐

My goal for this conference is to:

Questions/comments I have about my conference assignment:

I have completed this much of the current project so far. (Circle amount completed below.)

  Done 100%   90   80   70   60   50   40   30   20   10%   Not started

I have the following technical or computer-related problems or questions:

I have the following grammatical or writing process problems or questions:

News from my life you need to know which could affect my classroom performance:

One thing I could use some help understanding is:

Pre-Conference Form
(to be filled out before your conference)

introductory
composition
at purdue

08

English 106 Pre-Conference Preparation Notes

Date _____ / _____ / _____

Name _____ Group: A ☐ B ☐

My goal for this conference is to:

Questions/comments I have about my conference assignment:

I have completed this much of the current project so far. (Circle amount completed below.)

Done 100%   90   80   70   60   50   40   30   20   10%   Not started

I have the following technical or computer-related problems or questions:

I have the following grammatical or writing process problems or questions:

News from my life you need to know which could affect my classroom performance:

One thing I could use some help understanding is:

Pre-Conference Form
(to be filled out before your conference)

introductory
composition
at purdue

09

English 106 Pre-Conference Preparation Notes

Date _____/_____/_____

Name _____ Group: A ☐ B ☐

My goal for this conference is to:

Questions/comments I have about my conference assignment:

I have completed this much of the current project so far. (Circle amount completed below.)

Done 100%   90   80   70   60   50   40   30   20   10%   Not started

I have the following technical or computer-related problems or questions:

I have the following grammatical or writing process problems or questions:

News from my life you need to know which could affect my classroom performance:

One thing I could use some help understanding is:

10

English 106 Pre-Conference Preparation Notes

Date _____/_____/_____

Name _____   Group: A ☐   B ☐

My goal for this conference is to:

Questions/comments I have about my conference assignment:

I have completed this much of the current project so far. (Circle amount completed below.)

Done 100%   90   80   70   60   50   40   30   20   10%   Not started

I have the following technical or computer-related problems or questions:

I have the following grammatical or writing process problems or questions:

News from my life you need to know which could affect my classroom performance:

One thing I could use some help understanding is:

Pre-Conference Form
(to be filled out before your conference)

01

_____

English 106 Post-Conference Reflection

Date _____ / _____ / _____

Name _____ Group: A ☐   B ☐

My goal for this conference was met:

Fully ☐   Partially ☐   Not at all ☐

Assignments I still need to work on:

I notice that my writing is improving because I . . .

In my opinion, this conference was:

☐ Productive   ☐ Helpful
☐ Too long   ☐ Confusing
☐ Too short   ☐ Unnecessary
☐ _____   ☐ Just right
   Explain:

Items we did not discuss sufficiently that I still want to talk about:

Email the instructor with other comments or questions that occur to you outside of the conference times.

Please turn in your completed Conference Form at the next class period. Thank you for your input.

Post-Conference Form
(to be filled out after your conference)

02

English 106 Post-Conference Reflection

Date _____ / _____ / _____

Name _____   Group: A ☐   B ☐

My goal for this conference was met:

Fully ☐   Partially ☐   Not at all ☐

Assignments I still need to work on:

I notice that my writing is improving because I...

In my opinion, this conference was:

☐ Productive   ☐ Helpful
☐ Too long   ☐ Confusing
☐ Too short   ☐ Unnecessary
☐ _____ ☐ Just right
   Explain:

Items we did not discuss sufficiently that I still want to talk about:

Email the instructor with other comments or questions that occur to you outside of the conference times.

Please turn in your completed Conference Form at the next class period. Thank you for your input.

Post-Conference Form
(to be filled out after your conference)

introductory
composition
at purdue

03

English 106 Post-Conference Reflection

Date _____ / _____ / _____

Name _____ Group: A ☐ B ☐

My goal for this conference was met:

Fully ☐   Partially ☐   Not at all ☐

Assignments I still need to work on:

I notice that my writing is improving because I . . .

In my opinion, this conference was:

☐ Productive   ☐ Helpful
☐ Too long   ☐ Confusing
☐ Too short   ☐ Unnecessary
☐ _____ ☐ Just right
    Explain:

Items we did not discuss sufficiently that I still want to talk about:

Email the instructor with other comments or questions that occur to you outside of the conference times.

Please turn in your completed Conference Form at the next class period. Thank you for your input.

Post-Conference Form
(to be filled out after your conference)

introductory
composition
at purdue

04

English 106 Post-Conference Reflection

Date _____ / _____ / _____

Name _____   Group: A ☐   B ☐

My goal for this conference was met:

Fully ☐   Partially ☐   Not at all ☐

Assignments I still need to work on:

I notice that my writing is improving because I . . .

In my opinion, this conference was:

☐ Productive   ☐ Helpful
☐ Too long   ☐ Confusing
☐ Too short   ☐ Unnecessary
☐ _____   ☐ Just right
　 Explain:

Items we did not discuss sufficiently that I still want to talk about:

Email the instructor with other comments or questions that occur to you outside of the conference times.

Please turn in your completed Conference Form at the next class period. Thank you for your input.

Post-Conference Form
(to be filled out after your conference)

English 106 Post-Conference Reflection

Date   _____ / _____ / _____

Name   _____   Group: A ☐   B ☐

My goal for this conference was met:

Fully ☐   Partially ☐   Not at all ☐

Assignments I still need to work on:

I notice that my writing is improving because I . . .

In my opinion, this conference was:

☐ Productive   ☐ Helpful
☐ Too long   ☐ Confusing
☐ Too short   ☐ Unnecessary
☐ _____   ☐ Just right
   Explain:

Items we did not discuss sufficiently that I still want to talk about:

Email the instructor with other comments or questions that occur to you outside of the conference times.

Please turn in your completed Conference Form at the next class period. Thank you for your input.

Post-Conference Form
(to be filled out after your conference)

06

English 106 Post-Conference Reflection

Date _____/_____/_____

Name _____   Group: A ☐   B ☐

My goal for this conference was met:

Fully ☐   Partially ☐   Not at all ☐

Assignments I still need to work on:

I notice that my writing is improving because I . . .

In my opinion, this conference was:

☐ Productive   ☐ Helpful
☐ Too long   ☐ Confusing
☐ Too short   ☐ Unnecessary
☐ _____   ☐ Just right
    Explain:

Items we did not discuss sufficiently that I still want to talk about:

Email the instructor with other comments or questions that occur to you outside of the conference times.

Please turn in your completed Conference Form at the next class period. Thank you for your input.

Post-Conference Form
(to be filled out after your conference)

introductory
composition
at purdue

07

English 106 Post-Conference Reflection

Date _____/_____/_____

Name _____ Group: A ☐   B ☐

My goal for this conference was met:

Fully ☐   Partially ☐   Not at all ☐

Assignments I still need to work on:

I notice that my writing is improving because I...

In my opinion, this conference was:

☐ Productive   ☐ Helpful
☐ Too long   ☐ Confusing
☐ Too short   ☐ Unnecessary
☐ _____   ☐ Just right
      Explain:

Items we did not discuss sufficiently that I still want to talk about:

Email the instructor with other comments or questions that occur to you outside of the conference times.

Please turn in your completed Conference Form at the next class period. Thank you for your input.

Post-Conference Form
(to be filled out after your conference)

08

English 106 Post-Conference Reflection

Date _____ / _____ / _____

Name _____ Group: A ☐ B ☐

My goal for this conference was met:

Fully ☐ Partially ☐ Not at all ☐

Assignments I still need to work on:

I notice that my writing is improving because I . . .

In my opinion, this conference was:

☐ Productive ☐ Helpful
☐ Too long ☐ Confusing
☐ Too short ☐ Unnecessary
☐ _____ ☐ Just right
Explain:

Items we did not discuss sufficiently that I still want to talk about:

Email the instructor with other comments or questions that occur to you outside of the conference times.

Please turn in your completed Conference Form at the next class period. Thank you for your input.

Post-Conference Form
(to be filled out after your conference)

09

English 106 Post-Conference Reflection

Date _____ / _____ / _____

Name _____ Group: A ☐ B ☐

My goal for this conference was met:

Fully ☐ Partially ☐ Not at all ☐

Assignments I still need to work on:

I notice that my writing is improving because I . . .

In my opinion, this conference was:

☐ Productive   ☐ Helpful
☐ Too long   ☐ Confusing
☐ Too short   ☐ Unnecessary
☐ _____   ☐ Just right
    Explain:

Items we did not discuss sufficiently that I still want to talk about:

Email the instructor with other comments or questions that occur to you outside of the conference times.

Please turn in your completed Conference Form at the next class period. Thank you for your input.

Post-Conference Form
(to be filled out after your conference)

10

English 106 Post-Conference Reflection

Date _____ /_____ /_____

Name _____   Group: A ☐   B ☐

My goal for this conference was met:

Fully ☐   Partially ☐   Not at all ☐

Assignments I still need to work on:

I notice that my writing is improving because I...

In my opinion, this conference was:

☐ Productive   ☐ Helpful
☐ Too long   ☐ Confusing
☐ Too short   ☐ Unnecessary
☐ _____   ☐ Just right
        Explain:

Items we did not discuss sufficiently that I still want to talk about:

Email the instructor with other comments or questions that occur to you outside of the conference times.

Please turn in your completed Conference Form at the next class period. Thank you for your input.

Post-Conference Form
(to be filled out after your conference)

Peer Review A   1
RESPONDING TO PROJECT CRITERIA _____

Peer Review A focuses on the project criteria; therefore, you will carefully read and consider the work of your peers in light of the project guidelines. As a reviewer, your goal is to offer constructive, advice-centered comments that pair intuitive questions with productive suggestions. (Before beginning this peer review, please be sure you've read the section titled "Peer Review" on page 30.) Because this review will likely take place early in the composing process, it is not concerned with editing issues like spelling errors or grammar mistakes as long as these issues do not detract from the overall meaning of the project.

Project Writer: _____

Project Reviewer: _____

Step 1: Identifying the Project Criteria

Because this peer review will focus on the criteria for the project, you should spend time reading through your assignment guidelines with your instructor and classmates in order to list the project's major criteria below. These are the criteria that you will be looking for as you respond to your peer's work.

1.

2.

3.

4.

5.

Step 2: Reading to Understand the Project

Each person will be paired with a partner or group. Partners will exchange projects and take time to read over each other's work from beginning to end as an attempt to become acquainted with the project. During this reading, you should not mark on the project but rather read to be sure that you understand the main ideas being presented.

Step 3: Commenting on the Criteria

Next, partners will search for the criteria identified in Step 1. First, fill in Column 1 with the criteria. Then, as you notice the criteria throughout the assignment, use Column 2 to describe how well the project is meeting the criteria and use Column 3 to offer revision suggestions or questions. (Your partner will probably find sentences or phrases more useful than one word responses.) Keep in mind what the assignment is asking for and whether or not the project is meeting each criterion.

Criteria	Describe how well the project meets the criteria.	Explain any revisions you suggest and list any questions you have.
1		
2		
3		
4		
5		

Step 4: Discussion of Peer's Review and Writer's Plans

As the reviewer, discuss what you thought was working well and what suggestions you made for aspects that could be developed. Mention why you made those suggestions and how you think those suggestions could improve the overall direction of the project. Then, as the writer, discuss the advice that you think you are going to take. Explain what advice has been the most helpful and how will you attempt to revise the project with that advice in mind. (In addition to asking you to discuss your feedback, some instructors may ask you to write your revision plans.)

Peer Review A
RESPONDING TO PROJECT CRITERIA _____

Peer Review A focuses on the project criteria; therefore, you will carefully read and consider the work of your peers in light of the project guidelines. As a reviewer, your goal is to offer constructive, advice-centered comments that pair intuitive questions with productive suggestions. (Before beginning this peer review, please be sure you've read the section titled "Peer Review" on page 30.) Because this review will likely take place early in the composing process, it is not concerned with editing issues like spelling errors or grammar mistakes as long as these issues do not detract from the overall meaning of the project.

Project Writer: _____

Project Reviewer: _____

Step 1: Identifying the Project Criteria

Because this peer review will focus on the criteria for the project, you should spend time reading through your assignment guidelines with your instructor and classmates in order to list the project's major criteria below. These are the criteria that you will be looking for as you respond to your peer's work.

1.

2.

3.

4.

5.

Step 2: Reading to Understand the Project

Each person will be paired with a partner or group. Partners will exchange projects and take time to read over each other's work from beginning to end as an attempt to become acquainted with the project. During this reading, you should not mark on the project but rather read to be sure that you understand the main ideas being presented.

Step 3: Commenting on the Criteria

Next, partners will search for the criteria identified in Step 1. First, fill in Column 1 with the criteria. Then, as you notice the criteria throughout the assignment, use Column 2 to describe how well the project is meeting the criteria and use Column 3 to offer revision suggestions or questions. (Your partner will probably find sentences or phrases more useful than one word responses.) Keep in mind what the assignment is asking for and whether or not the project is meeting each criterion.

Criteria	Describe how well the project meets the criteria.	Explain any revisions you suggest and list any questions you have.
1		
2		
3		
4		
5		

Step 4: Discussion of Peer's Review and Writer's Plans

As the reviewer, discuss what you thought was working well and what suggestions you made for aspects that could be developed. Mention why you made those suggestions and how you think those suggestions could improve the overall direction of the project. Then, as the writer, discuss the advice that you think you are going to take. Explain what advice has been the most helpful and how will you attempt to revise the project with that advice in mind. (In addition to asking you to discuss your feedback, some instructors may ask you to write your revision plans.)

Peer Review A   3
Responding to Project Criteria _____

Peer Review A focuses on the project criteria; therefore, you will carefully read and consider the work of your peers in light of the project guidelines. As a reviewer, your goal is to offer constructive, advice-centered comments that pair intuitive questions with productive suggestions. (Before beginning this peer review, please be sure you've read the section titled "Peer Review" on page 30.) Because this review will likely take place early in the composing process, it is not concerned with editing issues like spelling errors or grammar mistakes as long as these issues do not detract from the overall meaning of the project.

Project Writer: _____

Project Reviewer: _____

Step 1: Identifying the Project Criteria

Because this peer review will focus on the criteria for the project, you should spend time reading through your assignment guidelines with your instructor and classmates in order to list the project's major criteria below. These are the criteria that you will be looking for as you respond to your peer's work.

1.

2.

3.

4.

5.

Step 2: Reading to Understand the Project

Each person will be paired with a partner or group. Partners will exchange projects and take time to read over each other's work from beginning to end as an attempt to become acquainted with the project. During this reading, you should not mark on the project but rather read to be sure that you understand the main ideas being presented.

Step 3: Commenting on the Criteria

Next, partners will search for the criteria identified in Step 1. First, fill in Column 1 with the criteria. Then, as you notice the criteria throughout the assignment, use Column 2 to describe how well the project is meeting the criteria and use Column 3 to offer revision suggestions or questions. (Your partner will probably find sentences or phrases more useful than one word responses.) Keep in mind what the assignment is asking for and whether or not the project is meeting each criterion.

Criteria	Describe how well the project meets the criteria.	Explain any revisions you suggest and list any questions you have.
1		
2		
3		
4		
5		

Step 4: Discussion of Peer's Review and Writer's Plans

As the reviewer, discuss what you thought was working well and what suggestions you made for aspects that could be developed. Mention why you made those suggestions and how you think those suggestions could improve the overall direction of the project. Then, as the writer, discuss the advice that you think you are going to take. Explain what advice has been the most helpful and how will you attempt to revise the project with that advice in mind. (In addition to asking you to discuss your feedback, some instructors may ask you to write your revision plans.)

Peer Review A   4
Responding to Project Criteria _____

Peer Review A focuses on the project criteria; therefore, you will carefully read and consider the work of your peers in light of the project guidelines. As a reviewer, your goal is to offer constructive, advice-centered comments that pair intuitive questions with productive suggestions. (Before beginning this peer review, please be sure you've read the section titled "Peer Review" on page 30.) Because this review will likely take place early in the composing process, it is not concerned with editing issues like spelling errors or grammar mistakes as long as these issues do not detract from the overall meaning of the project.

Project Writer: _____

Project Reviewer: _____

Step 1: Identifying the Project Criteria

Because this peer review will focus on the criteria for the project, you should spend time reading through your assignment guidelines with your instructor and classmates in order to list the project's major criteria below. These are the criteria that you will be looking for as you respond to your peer's work.

1.

2.

3.

4.

5.

Step 2: Reading to Understand the Project

Each person will be paired with a partner or group. Partners will exchange projects and take time to read over each other's work from beginning to end as an attempt to become acquainted with the project. During this reading, you should not mark on the project but rather read to be sure that you understand the main ideas being presented.

Step 3: Commenting on the Criteria

Next, partners will search for the criteria identified in Step 1. First, fill in Column 1 with the criteria. Then, as you notice the criteria throughout the assignment, use Column 2 to describe how well the project is meeting the criteria and use Column 3 to offer revision suggestions or questions. (Your partner will probably find sentences or phrases more useful than one word responses.) Keep in mind what the assignment is asking for and whether or not the project is meeting each criterion.

Criteria	Describe how well the project meets the criteria.	Explain any revisions you suggest and list any questions you have.
1		
2		
3		
4		
5		

Step 4: Discussion of Peer's Review and Writer's Plans

As the reviewer, discuss what you thought was working well and what suggestions you made for aspects that could be developed. Mention why you made those suggestions and how you think those suggestions could improve the overall direction of the project. Then, as the writer, discuss the advice that you think you are going to take. Explain what advice has been the most helpful and how will you attempt to revise the project with that advice in mind. (In addition to asking you to discuss your feedback, some instructors may ask you to write your revision plans.)

Peer Review A

5

RESPONDING TO PROJECT CRITERIA _____

Peer Review A focuses on the project criteria; therefore, you will carefully read and consider the work of your peers in light of the project guidelines. As a reviewer, your goal is to offer constructive, advice-centered comments that pair intuitive questions with productive suggestions. (Before beginning this peer review, please be sure you've read the section titled "Peer Review" on page 30.) Because this review will likely take place early in the composing process, it is not concerned with editing issues like spelling errors or grammar mistakes as long as these issues do not detract from the overall meaning of the project.

Project Writer: _____

Project Reviewer: _____

Step 1: Identifying the Project Criteria

Because this peer review will focus on the criteria for the project, you should spend time reading through your assignment guidelines with your instructor and classmates in order to list the project's major criteria below. These are the criteria that you will be looking for as you respond to your peer's work.

1.

2.

3.

4.

5.

Step 2: Reading to Understand the Project

Each person will be paired with a partner or group. Partners will exchange projects and take time to read over each other's work from beginning to end as an attempt to become acquainted with the project. During this reading, you should not mark on the project but rather read to be sure that you understand the main ideas being presented.

Step 3: Commenting on the Criteria

Next, partners will search for the criteria identified in Step 1. First, fill in Column 1 with the criteria. Then, as you notice the criteria throughout the assignment, use Column 2 to describe how well the project is meeting the criteria and use Column 3 to offer revision suggestions or questions. (Your partner will probably find sentences or phrases more useful than one word responses.) Keep in mind what the assignment is asking for and whether or not the project is meeting each criterion.

Criteria	Describe how well the project meets the criteria.	Explain any revisions you suggest and list any questions you have.
1		
2		
3		
4		
5		

Step 4: Discussion of Peer's Review and Writer's Plans

As the reviewer, discuss what you thought was working well and what suggestions you made for aspects that could be developed. Mention why you made those suggestions and how you think those suggestions could improve the overall direction of the project. Then, as the writer, discuss the advice that you think you are going to take. Explain what advice has been the most helpful and how will you attempt to revise the project with that advice in mind. (In addition to asking you to discuss your feedback, some instructors may ask you to write your revision plans.)

Peer Review B

4

PREPARING FINAL DRAFTS _____

Peer Review B focuses on preparing final drafts; therefore, you will carefully read and consider the work of your peers, noting the ways that they might polish this draft before submitting it. (Before beginning this peer review, please be sure you've read the section titled "Peer Review" on page 30.) Because this review will likely take place late in the composing process, it is concerned with stylistic and editing issues that can be revised once the writer has developed the overall content.

Project Writer: _____

Project Reviewer: _____

Step 1: Reading to Understand the Project

Each person will be paired with a partner or group. Partners will exchange projects and take time to read over each other's work from beginning to end in order to become acquainted with the project. During this reading, you should not mark on the project but rather read to be sure that you understand the overall topic.

Step 2: Commenting for Final Revisions

In this peer review, you will focus on the standard conventions for the genre and on elements of style and mechanics. You will make comments based on the four categories listed on the back of this sheet. Additionally, your instructor may ask you to comment on additional categories that are specific to your project. You can add these specific categories in numbers 4 and 5 on the back of this sheet.

Step3: Discussion of Peer's Review

Reviewer, after you've completed the prompts on the back of this sheet, discuss three revisions that you think will be most important as the writer prepares his or her final draft. Then, as the writer, discuss the advice that you think you are going to take. Explain what advice has been the most helpful and how will you attempt to revise the project with that advice in mind. (In addition to discussion, your instructor may ask you for **written revision plans** based on the feedback you've received.)

1. Based on your reading, who is the intended audience for the project? Describe the ways that the project meets the expectations of the intended audience?

2. Describe the ways that the project uses the standard conventions for the genre (i.e., if it is a narrative, how does it use the narrative conventions?).

3. Describe the ways that the citations are integrated. Are there sources that are not cited but should be? Are the sources appropriately cited for the format (i.e., MLA, APA, etc.) or genre?

4. Note any grammar, spelling, or punctuation errors. You may want to mark these directly on the draft and note them here.

5.

6.

Peer Review B   5
PREPARING FINAL DRAFTS _____

Peer Review B focuses on preparing final drafts; therefore, you will carefully read and consider the work of your peers, noting the ways that they might polish this draft before submitting it. (Before beginning this peer review, please be sure you've read the section titled "Peer Review" on page 30.) Because this review will likely take place late in the composing process, it is concerned with stylistic and editing issues that can be revised once the writer has developed the overall content.

Project Writer: _____

Project Reviewer: _____

Step 1: Reading to Understand the Project

Each person will be paired with a partner or group. Partners will exchange projects and take time to read over each other's work from beginning to end in order to become acquainted with the project. During this reading, you should not mark on the project but rather read to be sure that you understand the overall topic.

Step 2: Commenting for Final Revisions

In this peer review, you will focus on the standard conventions for the genre and on elements of style and mechanics. You will make comments based on the four categories listed on the back of this sheet. Additionally, your instructor may ask you to comment on additional categories that are specific to your project. You can add these specific categories in numbers 4 and 5 on the back of this sheet.

Step 3: Discussion of Peer's Review

Reviewer, after you've completed the prompts on the back of this sheet, discuss three revisions that you think will be most important as the writer prepares his or her final draft. Then, as the writer, discuss the advice that you think you are going to take. Explain what advice has been the most helpful and how will you attempt to revise the project with that advice in mind. (In addition to discussion, your instructor may ask you for **written revision plans** based on the feedback you've received.)

1. Based on your reading, who is the intended audience for the project? Describe the ways that the project meets the expectations of the intended audience?

2. Describe the ways that the project uses the standard conventions for the genre (i.e., if it is a narrative, how does it use the narrative conventions?).

3. Describe the ways that the citations are integrated. Are there sources that are not cited but should be? Are the sources appropriately cited for the format (i.e., MLA, APA, etc.) or genre?

4. Note any grammar, spelling, or punctuation errors. You may want to mark these directly on the draft and note them here.

5.

6.

ICaP Goals Chart

INDIVIDUAL WRITING PROJECT _____

Use the column to the right to describe which goals this project has met and how it has met these goals. (Remember each project does not need to meet all the goals; however, you should meet all of the goals by the end of the semester.)

ICaP
introductory
composition
at purdue

1

Rhetorical Knowledge	ICaP Goal	Project
	To understand the inherent rhetorical situation of writing including purpose, audience, and context.	
	To prepare for writing in later university courses across the curriculum by learning to articulate, develop, and support a point through both primary and secondary research.	
	To understand that writing can and should be used for multiple academic, civic, professional, and personal purposes.	

ICaP Goal	Project
To write as a means of discovery and learning; as an integral part of inquiry about shared material, social, and cultural contexts; and as a means of exploring, understanding, and evaluating ideas in academic disciplines.	
To develop abilities to create, interpret and evaluate a variety of types of texts integrating verbal and visual components.	

Critical Thinking, Reading, and Writing

ICaP Goals Chart
INDIVIDUAL WRITING PROJECT _____

2

Use the column to the right to describe which goals this project has met and how it has met these goals. (Remember each project does not need to meet all the goals; however, you should meet all of the goals by the end of the semester.)

ICaP Goal	Project
Rhetorical Knowledge	
To understand the inherent rhetorical situation of writing including purpose, audience, and context.	
To prepare for writing in later university courses across the curriculum by learning to articulate, develop, and support a point through both primary and secondary research.	
To understand that writing can and should be used for multiple academic, civic, professional, and personal purposes.	

ICaP Goal	Project
To write as a means of discovery and learning; as an integral part of inquiry about shared material, social, and cultural contexts; and as a means of exploring, understanding, and evaluating ideas in academic disciplines.	
To develop abilities to create, interpret and evaluate a variety of types of texts integrating verbal and visual components.	

Critical Thinking, Reading, and Writing

ICaP Goals Chart

INDIVIDUAL WRITING PROJECT _____

Use the column to the right to describe which goals this project has met and how it has met these goals. (Remember each project does not need to meet all the goals; however, you should meet all of the goals by the end of the semester.)

ICaP Goal	Project
Rhetorical Knowledge To understand the inherent rhetorical situation of writing including purpose, audience, and context.	
To prepare for writing in later university courses across the curriculum by learning to articulate, develop, and support a point through both primary and secondary research.	
To understand that writing can and should be used for multiple academic, civic, professional, and personal purposes.	

ICaP Goal	Project
To write as a means of discovery and learning; as an integral part of inquiry about shared material, social, and cultural contexts; and as a means of exploring, understanding, and evaluating ideas in academic disciplines.	
To develop abilities to create, interpret and evaluate a variety of types of texts integrating verbal and visual components.	

Critical Thinking, Reading, and Writing

ICaP Goals Chart

INDIVIDUAL WRITING PROJECT _____

Use the column to the right to describe which goals this project has met and how it has met these goals. (Remember each project does not need to meet all the goals; however, you should meet all of the goals by the end of the semester.)

	ICaP Goal	Project
Rhetorical Knowledge	To understand the inherent rhetorical situation of writing including purpose, audience, and context.	
	To prepare for writing in later university courses across the curriculum by learning to articulate, develop, and support a point through both primary and secondary research.	
	To understand that writing can and should be used for multiple academic, civic, professional, and personal purposes.	

4

ICaP Goal	Project
To write as a means of discovery and learning; as an integral part of inquiry about shared material, social, and cultural contexts; and as a means of exploring, understanding, and evaluating ideas in academic disciplines.	
To develop abilities to create, interpret and evaluate a variety of types of texts integrating verbal and visual components.	

Critical Thinking, Reading, and Writing

ICaP Goals Chart

INDIVIDUAL WRITING PROJECT _____

Use the column to the right to describe which goals this project has met and how it has met these goals. (Remember each project does not need to meet all the goals; however, you should meet all of the goals by the end of the semester.)

icap
introductory
composition
at purdue

5

	ICaP Goal	Project
Rhetorical Knowledge	To understand the inherent rhetorical situation of writing including purpose, audience, and context.	
	To prepare for writing in later university courses across the curriculum by learning to articulate, develop, and support a point through both primary and secondary research.	
	To understand that writing can and should be used for multiple academic, civic, professional, and personal purposes.	

ICaP Goal	Project
Critical Thinking, Reading, and Writing	
To write as a means of discovery and learning; as an integral part of inquiry about shared material, social, and cultural contexts; and as a means of exploring, understanding, and evaluating ideas in academic disciplines.	
To develop abilities to create, interpret and evaluate a variety of types of texts integrating verbal and visual components.	

ICaP Goals Chart

COURSE OVERVIEW

Use the columns to the right to describe which goals each project has met and how it met this goal. (Remember each project does not need to meet all the goals.)

ICaP Goal	Project	Project	Project	Project
Rhetorical Knowledge				
To understand the inherent rhetorical situation of writing including purpose, audience, and context.				
To prepare for writing in later university courses across the curriculum by learning to articulate, develop, and support a point through both primary and secondary research.				
To understand that writing can and should be used for multiple academic, civic, professional, and personal purposes.				

ICaP Goal	Project	Project	Project	Project
To write as a means of discovery and learning; as an integral part of inquiry about shared material, social, and cultural contexts; and as a means of exploring, understanding, and evaluating ideas in academic disciplines.				
To develop abilities to create, interpret and evaluate a variety of types of texts integrating verbal and visual components.				

Critical Thinking, Reading, and Writing